Thematic Research Projects

Powerful Tools to Organize and Assess Research

Paula Hertel
Patricia Ward

Rigby Best Teachers Press

An imprint of Rigby

For more information about other books from Rigby Best Teachers Press, please contact Rigby at 1-800-822-8661 or visit **www.rigby.com**

Editors: Bobbie Dempsey and Carol Allison
Executive Editor: Georgine Cooper
Designer: Biner Design
Design Production Manager: Tom Sjoerdsma
Cover Design: Ann Cain
Cover Illustrator: David Merrill
Interior Illustrator: Yoshi Miyake
Photo Credits: All photos © PhotoDisc, except for forest on page 13 and hieroglyphs on pages 119-139 © Artville.

07 06 05 04 03 02
10 9 8 7 6 5 4 3 2 1

Printed in the United States of America.

ISBN 0-7635-7752-9
Thematic Research Projects: Powerful Tools to Organize and Assess Research

Preface

Elementary students are naturally curious and need to learn strategies to research and organize data. As learning develops, students move from fact finding to interpretation and meaningful presentation of newfound knowledge.

Reading and language arts skills, such as letter writing, note taking, and outlining, must be integrated throughout the content areas in order for students to truly understand their applications. Students need to observe and practice creative ways to present data and expository writing. Students need to discover that many pieces of literature can be companions to reference materials, offering different points of view on a subject. Project guidelines, data collectors, and graphic organizers are tools students can use to further the research process.

Because students have varied learning styles, multiple intelligences, and different levels of knowledge, teachers need to encourage them to apply as many abilities as possible. We should offer ways for them to do collaborative and independent research in order to give students support at their levels of ability. We should introduce students to the wide variety of resources, including textbooks and reference materials, available to them. Resources include trade books, videos, magazines, newspapers, interviews, and the world of technology, such as CD-ROMs, the Internet, and interactive learning venues.

It is important for students to tap into their own creativity as they share and communicate what they have learned. Different student learning styles lead to different presentation styles, such as poetry, reports, posters, skits, music, models, presentation software, and video taping. These choices allow students to share their knowledge and enjoy the presentation process while informing others.

When assessing students' work, consider the skills and knowledge they have learned in the content areas. Rubrics, also called *performance scoring guides* or *assessment keys*, are included with each topic and offer a way for the student and teacher to measure progress. Assessment should be fluid and tailored to the specific educational setting. However, not all activities require a rubric or formal assessment. Some assignments are designed to develop the learning process, acquire information, or express information in a different way.

Finally, the processes of group and individual reflection are essential. All students can perceive learning as a journey, enjoying where they have been and anticipating their next adventure.

Paula Hertel and Patricia Ward

Contents

Introduction

Science Themes

Characteristics of the rain forest and the animals that inhabit these regions

Physical geographical regions and their characteristics

Endangered species and the why these animals are at risk

Similarities and differences between insects and arachnids

Famous inventors and their inventions

How and why natural disasters occur

Social Studies Themes

Introduction

How to Use This Book

Thematic Research Project: Powerful Tools to Organize and Assess Research was developed for classroom teachers, by classroom teachers, for use with students in grades 4-8. These field-tested reproducible research tools will assist you in:

- teaching the steps of research to your students

- assessing the products and presentations that arise from that research.

This teacher resource has twelve units that can be adapted to meet the needs of your students. They are grouped into two categories and can be used in any order. You can implement these topics within an existing curriculum structure or use them to individualize assignments to meet the needs of your students.

Each unit offers a *Main Assignment* and *Extension Activities*. The *Extension Activities* offer a variety of presentation strategies for students to share what they have learned. You can adapt any presentation idea for use with a whole class, small group, and/or individual students. Feel free to add or delete activities from the assignments. The research process in this book helps students to move from fact finding, through interpretation, to meaningful and creative presentations that inform others.

Research Tools

To help carry out this process, each unit includes reproducible *Tools* to guide students to think, search, process, present, and evaluate information in a systematic way. Discuss all tools with students before research begins.

- **Main Assignment and Extensions** introduce the *Main Assignment* and *Extension Activities* and give students opportunities to share what they have learned.

- **Graphic Organizers** help students gather and organize information.

Research Tools

- **Data Collectors** help students expand notetaking to interpretation.

- **Guidelines** explain the steps required in a research presentation project.

- **Rubrics** assess the process of research and the final product. These also allow you and the student to share a common understanding of what is required to do the best job on a project.

- **Student Observation of Oral Presentations** ask students to assess how a fellow student shares information.

- **Reflection Forms** are used by students at the end of a unit so that they may practice metacognition–thinking about where they have been and what new steps will further their learning.

- **Group Evaluations** help students become aware of the skills required to accomplish a task as a member of a group. The *Group Evaluation* lists nine items by which each group can determine its success in a cooperative learning situation.

Cooperative Grouping

In a class where cooperative learning is implemented, it is the teacher's job to:

- Select a heterogeneous group of three to five students

- Assist the groups in determining the task to be completed

- Set the daily time period for work to be accomplished

- Set the same behavioral expectations and consequences for small groups that you would expect for any whole-class activity

Thematic Unit Guidelines

Following are the steps for implementing any of the units in *Thematic Research Projects:*

- Review the introductory pages, which include *Unit Goals, Memo to the Teacher,* and *Materials and Resources* for the unit.

- With the help of the school librarian and the students, gather the materials and resources needed for the research. Website suggestions are provided. ***Rigby is not responsible for the content of any website listed in the Internet Resources section of each unit. All material is the responsibility of the hosts and creators.***

- Reproduce the *Student Research Guidelines* and *Report Guidelines.* Distribute copies to each student. Allow time in class to discuss guidelines for research and report writing.

- Clarify the expectations of the *Main Assignment* by reading the *Student Projects* page for the product or presentation with the group. Hand out the *Research Tools* that your students will need to complete their research and presentations.

- Select *Extension Activities* based on several variables, such as time, maturity level of students, and available resources.

- Discuss *Rubrics* with students as they begin research projects to provide clear understanding of expectations.

- Three to five students will constitute each cooperative grouping or learning team for a small group activity. Choose students for each group based on a range of learning abilities and make sure students' skills complement one another.

- Set aside at least 45 minutes for each research session. The number of days or weeks required to complete research depends on the learning level of the students and the topic selected.

- Students begin the research process by reading, listening, and gathering information to complete the *Graphic Organizer.* Encourage students to delve into the topic and to take notes.

Thematic Unit Guidelines

Introduction

- To express their understandings beyond basic notetaking, students should provide details and description and write in complete sentences on the *Data Collector* form.

- To meet individual needs or to support skill development at particular stages of research, use your discretion to choose which *Tools* are appropriate. Be available to help the students with key parts of the research process and offer guidance and support as presentations are developed.

- After gathering the data, students create a research-based presentation that follows the *Student Project Guidelines.* This can be in the form of a poem, report, model, video, play, and so on.

- Students can use previously collected data or add new data to complete the *Extension Activities*.

- Students will display or present information to an audience, such as classmates, parents, and other classes.

- Complete one *Rubric* per student to assess each student's performance. Circle the number of the paragraph that best describes the student's performance on a continuum of 4 (highest) to 1 (lowest). This performance assessment is useful for showing the student his or her strengths and the areas where future improvements can be made. File *Rubrics* for follow up conferences.

It is important to remember that there are many ways to apply the ideas offered in this book, based on your teaching style and the learning styles of your students. Use these *Tools* as models for developing your own for future research projects. Above all, have fun with the process!

Student Research Guidelines

- Select the topic for your research. Ask your teacher for help if you need it.

- Use the materials your teacher has selected to find information about your topic, including books, periodicals, encyclopedias, CD-ROMs, the Internet, and so on.

- Use a Graphic Organizer to take notes from these resources.

- Use a Data Collector to develop the details of your research from your notes. Write answers in complete sentences and write more than one sentence when appropriate. You may refer to your sources of information, but do not copy phrases or sentences.

- Review the Main Assignment requirements with your teacher.

- If there is a Rubric for the project, review it before you begin the project to understand how you will be assessed.

- Follow the Guidelines to complete the Main Assignment and any Extension Activity.

- If you have been part of a cooperative group activity, fill in and discuss the Group Evaluation with your group and your teacher.

- Share and celebrate your completed project(s) with the class.

- Use the Reflection Form to write about how and what you have learned.

Introduction

From time to time, you will be asked to write a report using the information you have found in your research. Every report should consist of a title page, at least five paragraphs of text, and a bibliography. Following is more information on writing each of these elements for your report.

Title Page

The title page of a report is its front page. Center the title of the report and your name in the top 1/3 of the title page. Your teacher's name, the date on which the report is due, and any other information your teacher asks you to include, should be centered in the lower 1/3 of the page. Here is an example of a completed title page. Remember that title pages are always neatly hand written, typed, or word processed.

> The Evolution
> of Toasters
> By Samson Lee
>
>
> Grade 6
> Mrs. Lieberman
> January 22, 2004

Report Text

The text of a report consists of five paragraphs or more. Following is a description of each paragraph:

- The *first paragraph* introduces your topic and generally lists the three main points about it. Main points are mentioned in the order in which they will appear in the next three paragraphs.

- The *second paragraph* identifies one point about your topic and explains more about it.

- The *third paragraph* identifies a second point about your topic and explains more about it.

- The *fourth paragraph* identifies a third point about your topic and explains more about it.

- The *fifth paragraph* explains why you chose this particular topic. Your research has helped you to become knowledgeable about this topic. Demonstrate how much you have learned. This paragraph ends with a sentence that states your conclusions or provides a quote on the topic by an expert.

Introduction

Attention to Detail

- Edit for:

  Capitalization (sentence beginnings, proper nouns, titles)

  Understanding (makes sense)

  Punctuation (periods, commas, exclamation points, question marks)

  Spelling (spell check or use a dictionary)

- Include a title page, bibliography page, and your Graphic Organizer and Data Collector.

Bibliography

A bibliography is an alphabetical list of the resources used in your research.

Bibliography Format:

- Author or editor (last name first, then first name)

- Title of work (Book and magazine titles are underlined or in italics, magazine articles are in quotes.)

- City of publication: publisher, date published
  (Show page numbers if you used part of a book instead of the entire work.)

- The entry always ends with a period.

Examples:

Norwich, John Julius. *Great Architecture of the World*, New York: Bonanza Books, 1983 (34-41).

Ottinger, John. "Chasing Down the Cuban Crocodile," *National Geographic World*, July, 2001 (8-11).

Science
Themes

1 • Animals of the Rain Forest

Memo to the Teacher

You can teach this unit in conjunction with an overall study of the rain forest. Students should first choose an animal of the rain forest and begin researching that animal. Included are suggested choices that students can use to enhance their research.

At the end of the research phase of the activity, students will create a slide show presentation showcasing what they have learned about their animals. This presentation can be created by individual students or small groups. After viewing a presentation, complete the rubric provided by circling the choice in each row that applies to each student's or group's work. Meet with the student or group to share the rubric.

If students worked on a project in a cooperative group, they should complete the Group Evaluation together. This evaluation offers students the opportunity to assess the effectiveness of their group by focusing on what worked and what might need improvement. Students fill out the evaluation and share their responses as a group and with you.

At the end of the unit, the students fill out a Reflection Form to encourage individual learners to think about how and what they have learned. Students write their responses to the questions to share with the class. File evaluations for use during parent conferences.

After students finish the main assignment, you may add to, delete, or require one or more of the extension activities as part of the unit. Many of the extensions also include assessment rubrics.

If you do not have slide show presentation software, or your students do not have access to computers, use an extension activity as your main assignment.

★ Unit Goals

Content Objective:
Become familiar with an animal of the rain forest and understand the effects of environment on that animal's survival.

Performance Objective:
Use the information gathered to create a presentation using slide show presentation software that showcases the animal.

Materials and Resources

Main Assignment

Each student or group needs one copy of each of the following:
- Main Assignment and Extensions
- Graphic Organizer (3 pages)
- Data Collector (2 pages)
- Slide Show Presentation Guidelines
- Slide Show Presentation Planner (4 copies per student)
- Slide Show Presentation Rubric
- Group Evaluation
- Reflection Form

Extension Activities

If students pursue additional activities, each student will need one copy of each of the following:

Create an Animal Perspective Poem
- Animal's Perspective Poem Guidelines

Design a Diorama of the Animal in Its Habitat
- Diorama Guidelines
- Diorama Rubric

Develop a Board Game for Animals of the Rain Forest
- Board Game Guidelines
- Board Game Rubric

Internet Resources

The Electronic Zoo:
    http://netvet.wustl.edu/e-zoo.htm

Animals of the Rain Forest:
    http://www.animalsoftherainforest.com/frames.htm

Student Projects

Main Assignment

Collect data about an animal that lives in the rain forest.

Examples include, but are not limited to the following:

parrot	chameleon	gibbon
sloth	boa constrictor	gecko
tree frog	toucan	iguana
jaguar	orangutan	cobra
macaw	chimpanzee	anteater
anaconda	mandrill	tapir

When you have finished your research, use the information you have found to create a slide show presentation about the animal.

Extension Activities

After completing the main assignment, show what you have learned by completing one of the following extension activities. Your teacher will give you more information about each activity and will ask you to work independently, in a small group, or with the whole class.

1. Create a poem written from a rain forest animal's perspective.

2. Create a diorama of the rain forest animal in its habitat.

3. Create a board game about animals of the rain forest.

4. Other Activity: _____

Name _____   **Date** _____

1 • Animals of the Rain Forest

(**Rain forest layer**)

(**Plants and animals found in this layer**)

Rain forest animal

(**Natural habitat**)

(**Diet**)

Name   **Date**

1 • Animals of the Rain Forest

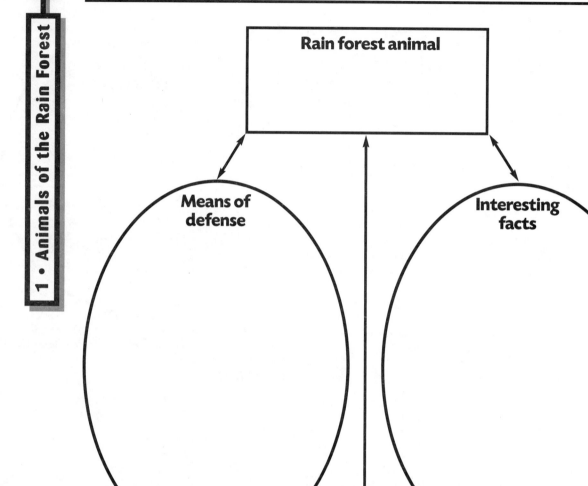

Rain forest animal

Means of defense

Interesting facts

Adaptive physical characteristics

Name _____ **Date** _____

1 • Animals of the Rain Forest

How is your animal helpful to humans?

_____
_____
_____
_____
_____
_____
_____
_____
_____

How is your animal harmful to humans?

_____
_____
_____
_____
_____
_____
_____
_____
_____

List titles and authors of resources used:

_____
_____
_____
_____
_____
_____
_____
_____
_____

Data Collector, Part 1

Name _____ **Date** _____

Name of the animal:

_____

Where is the animal's habitat located?

_____

What layer of the rain forest does the animal inhabit?

_____

What plants and animals are found in this layer of the rain forest?

_____

_____

Describe the physical characteristics of the animal.

_____

_____

_____

What physical features allow the animal to adapt to its environment?

_____

_____

_____

Describe the animal's eating habits?

_____

_____

_____

How does the animal defend itself?

_____

_____

1 • Animals of the Rain Forest

Name _____ **Date** _____

Who or what are the animal's enemies?

_____

_____

How is your animal helpful and/or harmful to nature, humans, or other creatures?

_____

_____

_____

List two interesting facts about your rain forest animal.

_____

_____

_____

List the book titles and authors you used to find your information.

_____

_____

_____

_____

Draw a sketch of your animal in its natural habitat.

Main Assignment • Slide Show Presentation

Slide Show Presentation Guidelines

After collecting data about your rain forest animal, create a slide show presentation that showcases a rain forest animal.

Use these tips to help you create your presentation:

- The slide show presentation should include at least 10 slides.

- The presentation should include a creative title slide with the title of the presentation and the name(s) of the author(s) of the presentation.

- The presentation should include most of the information from your data collector or graphic organizer. Write the information in complete sentences and include illustrations or clip art. (Remember that the purpose of this presentation is to inform and to entertain.)

- The final slide should contain a list of books and authors that you used to research the information in the presentation.

- All slides should contain buttons.

- The presentation should be easy to navigate.

Name _____ **Date** _____

Use this sheet to help you plan your slide show presentation.

1 • Animals of the Rain Forest

Slide # _____
Text _____

Slide # _____
Text _____

Slide # _____
Text _____

Main Assignment • Slide Show Rubric

Name _____ **Date** _____

Project Title _____ **Total** _____

Circle the number of the paragraph that best describes the student's performance on a continuum of 4 (highest) to 1 (lowest).

	4	**3**	**2**	**1**
Overall Presentation	Project demonstrates high-level mastery of the topic. Presentation is varied and flows well. Project is unique and shows a high level of creativity.	Project demonstrates mastery of the topic. Presentation is varied, creative, and interesting.	Project demonstrates limited mastery of the topic. Presentation is somewhat disjointed and hard to follow.	Project demonstrates little or no understanding of the topic. Presentation lacks cohesiveness and is difficult to follow and comprehend.
Visuals (Video Presentation)	The visuals enhance the topic and offer an original interpretation of information.	Visuals were effectively used and presented in an inventive manner.	Visuals demonstrate limited creativity. The presentation shows an attempt to expand the ideas of the topic.	Visuals show lack of creativity. The presentation is fragmented and distracts from the content of the topic.
Computer Presentation	Presentation demonstrates high-level knowledge of topic ideas and concepts and flows well. Tools and buttons are used correctly and creatively.	Knowledge of the topic is evident. The presentation is easy to follow and understand. Buttons and tools are used correctly.	An attempt has been made to include the basic fundamentals of slide show design.	The presentation is difficult to understand. Buttons and tools are improperly used.
Use of Technology	Demonstrates high level of understanding and comfort with the technology used in the project. Technology communicates topic ideas effectively.	Demonstrates understanding of the technology used. Technology is used effectively to demonstrate knowledge about the topic.	Demonstrates limited understanding of the technology. Technology used shows an attempt to communicate knowledge of the topic.	Project demonstrates little or no knowledge of the technology used. Knowledge of content is lost in the process.

 Animal's Perspective Poem Guidelines

Use the information that you have collected about a rain forest animal to complete the following:

Title (name of the animal)

_____

Line 1: I live in (animal's natural and geographic habitat),

_____

Line 2: Surrounded by (description of the habitat or environment).

_____

Line 3: I hunt (kinds of foods it eats).

_____

Line 4: I fear (animal's enemies).

_____

Line 5: I am (name of the animal).

_____

Example:

The Jaguar

I live in the tropical rain forest of South America,
Surrounded by tall grasses and green trees.
I hunt spider monkeys and sloths.
I fear the loss of my habitat.
I am the jaguar.

 # Diorama Guidelines

Use the information you have gathered to create a diorama that showcases your animal in its rain forest environment.

To make a diorama, follow these guidelines:

- Use a shoebox or similar cardboard container for the diorama.

- Use construction paper, paints, crayons, and/or markers to create a background (habitat) for the diorama.

- Create the animal from clay, construction paper, or your choice of materials. Be creative.

- Be sure to make the diorama reflect the emergent, canopy, and ground layers found in the rain forest. Place the animal in the correct layer.

- If you add other animals to the diorama, be sure they are placed in the correct rain forest layer.

- Use scrap materials, such as twigs and string, to enhance the diorama.

- Include a 3-inch-by-5-inch index card with a detailed description of the diorama.

- Make the diorama appealing and attractive.

1 • Animals of the Rain Forest

Extension Activity • Diorama Rubric

Name _____ **Date** _____

Project Title _____ **Total** _____

Circle the number of the paragraph that best describes the student's performance on a continuum of 4 (highest) to 1 (lowest).

1 • Animals of the Rain Forest

	4	3	2	1
Evidence of Research	The diorama demonstrates high level of knowledge about the animal and its habitat. The description of the model is unique and creative.	The diorama demonstrates mastery of the topic. The diorama replicates the animal and its habitat. The description offers details about both.	The diorama demonstrates limited understanding of the rain forest animal. The description contains few details about the animal and its habitat.	The model demonstrates little or no understanding of the topic. The description fails to be informative.
Construction	The diorama represents a detailed understanding of the topic.	The diorama demonstrates some knowledge about a rain forest animal and its environment.	The model attempts to represent some aspect of the topic.	The diorama demonstrates little knowledge of the topic. It is poorly constructed and messy.
Creative Use of Materials and Color	The diorama shows a high level of creativity in the use of materials and design.	The diorama is creative and interesting. Color, style, and artistic presentation are evident.	The diorama shows limited creativity.	The diorama shows a lack of creativity.
Presentation	The diorama enhances the topic and is highly appealing and attractive.	The diorama is attractive, pleasing to the eye, and representative of the topic.	The diorama shows an attempt to represent the basic requirements of the project guidelines.	The model is messy and not pleasing to look at.

Board Game Guidelines

Work in a small group of three to four students to develop a board game about animals of the rain forest.

Follow these guidelines:

- The purpose of the board game is to teach others about animals of the rain forest.

- The board game should have a catchy, unique title.

- The rules of the game should be easy to understand and follow.

- The game should include at least three different animals. The game should have at least 20 questions with answers.

- The board game should be attractive and inviting.

1 • Animals of the Rain Forest

Extension Activity • Board Game Rubric

Name _____ **Date** _____

Project Title _____ **Total** _____

Circle the number of the paragraph that best describes the student's performance on a continuum of 4 (highest) to 1 (lowest).

	4	3	2	1
Overall Game	The game demonstrates high level of mastery about rain forest animals. The game rules are easy to understand and easy to follow.	The board game increases others' knowledge about rain forest animals. The game illustrates important topic details and/or concepts.	The game demonstrates limited mastery of the topic. The game poorly represents topic ideas.	The game demonstrates little or no understanding of the topic. The game rules are difficult to understand and follow.
Game Board	The board game shows a high level of creativity. Project demonstrates high-level knowledge of topic ideas and concepts.	The game board is creative and interesting. Knowledge of the rain forest is evident.	The game board demonstrates limited creativity. The board game attempts to represent some aspect of the topic.	The game board shows lack of creativity. It is poorly constructed. The board game demonstrates little knowledge of the topic.
Creative Use of Materials and Color	Creative use of materials and color is evident.	Color, style, and artistic presentation are evident.	The game demonstrates some creative use of materials.	The game demonstrates little creative use of materials.
Attractive and Inviting	The board game is inviting and attractive. The game enhances others' knowledge of rain forest animals. The game is fun to play.	The game is attractive, pleasing to the eye, and representative of the topic concepts.	An attempt has been made to include the basic requirements of the game.	The game is messy and not pleasing to look at.

Group Evaluation

Name _____ **Date** _____

Group Name _____ **Total** _____

Fill in the blank next to each statement below with the following numbers: 4, 3, 2, or 1. Use the numbers to indicate how well the group worked together.

> **4** Very best efforts were given each time we met.
> **3** Good effort was given each time we met.
> **2** Some effort was shown, but direction was needed from outside the group.
> **1** Little effort was given to the project.

Group Members:

_____ Showed positive behavior.

_____ Cooperated by listening to each other.

_____ Shared creative ideas.

_____ Used good organizational skills.

_____ Contributed good research to develop the project.

_____ Brought and/or shared materials when needed.

_____ Cleaned up materials at the end of each work session.

_____ Produced an attractive, neat, and accurate project.

_____ Planned the presentation together, with all members taking part.

Please add any comments about the cooperative behavior of your group that you feel would be helpful for your teacher to know.

_____

_____

_____

_____

Reflection Form

1 • Animals of the Rain Forest

Name _____ **Date** _____

I enjoyed learning about . . .
_____
_____
_____

I especially enjoyed doing . . .
_____
_____
_____

I am still wondering about . . .
_____
_____
_____

The materials in which I found the most information were . . .
_____
_____
_____

What I found most challenging was . . .
_____
_____
_____

I improved the most in . . .
_____
_____
_____

2 • Biomes and Landforms of the Earth

Memo to the Teacher

A list of the geographic terms with definitions is included in this unit. Review these terms with students to be sure that everyone can read and understand the vocabulary. You can add to or delete from the list of terms, depending on your curriculum requirements. Provide your students with resources that clarify the visual representations of these geographic forms.

At the end of the research phase, students will develop a triorama showing what they have learned about the geography concepts they researched. The triorama should include an image and written definition of each biome, with the appropriate water and landforms for that area. The triorama can be created by individual students or small groups.

After viewing a presentation, complete the rubric provided by circling the choice in each row that applies to each student's or group's work. Meet with students to share the completed rubric.

If students worked on a project in a cooperative group, they should complete the Group Evaluation together. This evaluation offers students the opportunity to assess the effectiveness of their group by focusing on what worked and what might need improvement. Students are to fill out the forms and share their responses.

At the end of the unit, students will fill out a Reflection Form to encourage individual learners to think about how and what they have learned. Students write their responses to the questions to share with the class. File evaluations for use during parent conferences.

After students finish the main assignment, you may add to, delete, or require one or more of the extension activities. Many of the extensions include assessment rubrics.

★ Unit Goals

Content Objective:
Develop an understanding of plant and animal communities covering large geographical regions (biomes) and their various physical features (landforms and bodies of water).

Performance Objective:
Use the information gathered to develop a triorama for display.

Materials and Resources

Main Assignment

Each student or group needs one copy of each of the following:

- Main Assignment
- Study Sheet - Biomes
- Study Sheet - Landforms and Bodies of Water
- Triorama Guidelines
- Graphic Organizer (1 page)
- Data Collector (2 pages)
- Triorama Rubric
- Group Evaluation
- Reflection Form

✏ Extension Activities

If students pursue additional activities, each student will need one copy of each of the following:

Research Your Favorite Biome
- Research Guidelines
- Data Collector
- My Favorite Biome Rubric

Create a Geography Game Show
- Game Show Guidelines

Write a Geography Poem
- Geography Poem Guidelines

Internet Resources

The World's Biomes:
> http://www.ucmp.berkeley.edu/glossary/gloss5/biome/

Water Bodies:
> http://geography.about.com/science/geography/library/misc/
> blwaterbodies.htm

Student Projects

Main Assignment

Research biomes and various landforms and bodies of water listed in the unit glossary. When you finish your research, use the information to create a triorama with images and descriptions of one biome and its related landforms and bodies of water.

Extension Activities

After you complete the main assignment, show what you have learned by completing one of the following extension activities. Your teacher will provide more information about each activity and ask you to work independently, in a small group, or with the whole class.

1. Write a report about your favorite biome.

2. Create a geography game show.

3. Write a geography poem.

4. Other Activity: _____

Study Sheet 1: Biomes Glossary

A **biome** is a plant and animal community covering a large geographical area. An area is usually defined as a biome by its climate. The same biome may be found on several different continents. Following is a list of major land biomes:

boreal forest or taiga– An area covered thickly with coniferous trees, found in colder regions, such as near the tundra of Russia or Alaska.

chaparral– An area with many low, thorny bushes that can be rainy or hot and dry as in the southwestern United States.

desert– A barren area, usually thorny and without trees, that is hot and has little or no rainfall, as in the southwestern United States and Egypt.

grasslands– An area with much grass, few trees, and generally temperate weather, as in the Plains of the United States.

savanna– A level, grassy area with few or no trees, lying near deserts or tropical forests, as in the southeastern United States or western Africa.

temperate coniferous forest– An area covered thickly with trees, found in middle and upper mountain regions, that experiences a great deal of rain and mild winters, as in the Pacific Northwest of the United States.

temperate deciduous forest– An area covered thickly with trees, found in regions with cold winters and hot summers that cause the trees to lose their leaves, as in the Eastern and Midwestern regions of the United States.

tropical rain forest– An area of dense vegetation found near the equator that is always warm and wet, as in South America.

tundra– A large, level, treeless area in an arctic or high mountain region, as in Alaska and northern Canada. The ground underneath the tundra is always frozen.

Landforms and Bodies of Water

bay– part of an ocean or lake that is partly enclosed by land; usually smaller than a gulf

canyon– a narrow valley with high, steep sides, usually with a stream at the bottom

coast– land that borders on the sea or ocean

delta– deposits of earth and sand that collect at the mouth of a river; usually three-sided

glacier– a huge body of ice that moves slowly over land

gulf– an arm of the ocean or sea extending into the land; a large bay

hill– a raised part of the land, but smaller than a mountain

island– an area of land surrounded by water

lake– a body of water, usually fresh, almost or entirely surrounded by land

mountain– a very steep, high elevation of the Earth's surface

mountain range– a group of connected, steep, high land areas

mouth of a river– the place where a river flows into a larger body of water

ocean– an entire body of salt water that covers almost three-fourths of the Earth's surface

peninsula– a piece of land that is surrounded by water on three sides

plain– a broad stretch of level or nearly level land

plateau– a large level area of high land

river– a large natural stream of water that flows into a lake, an ocean, or another river

source of a river– the place where a river begins

strait– a narrow waterway that connects two larger bodies of water

tributary– a stream or small river that flows into a larger river

valley– a wide region of lowlands lying between hills or mountains; a stream or river may flow through it

volcano– a cone-shaped hill or mountain that was built up from steam, rocks, ashes, and lava shooting up through a vent in the Earth's crust

waterfall– water dropping or flowing from a high place in hills or mountains

Name _____

Date _____

2 · Biomes and Landforms of the Earth

Biome: _____

Description: _____

Bodies of Water

Landforms

Data Collector, Part 1

Name _____ **Date** _____

Name of biome:

_____

In what areas of the world is this biome found?

_____

_____

_____

What is the climate like in this biome throughout the year?

_____

_____

_____

_____

What type of animal life exists there?

_____

_____

_____

_____

What types of vegetation exist there?

_____

_____

_____

_____

What characteristics of this biome support or do not support human and animal life?

_____

_____

_____

_____

Name _____ **Date** _____

2 • Biomes and Landforms of the Earth

Interesting facts about this biome.

_____

_____

_____

_____

_____

_____

_____

_____

_____

_____

_____

_____

Draw a sketch of this biome.

2 • Biomes and Landforms of the Earth

i Triorama Guidelines

The triorama allows you to display many pictures and cutouts on the inside and outside of its folded paper.

To create a triorama, follow these directions:

- Use a 12-inch-by-12-inch square piece of construction paper, any color.

- Fold the paper diagonally in both directions. Make both folds inward, so that when you are finished and open the paper again, the paper almost looks like a bowl.

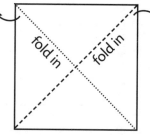

- Cut along one fold from the corner to the middle of the paper.

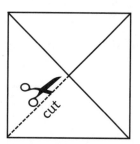

- You now have four triangles. Fold the paper in half along the uncut line.

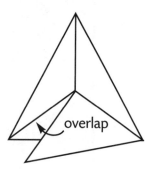

- At the cut, fold one triangle over the other to create a base. Tape or glue the base closed.

You are now ready to use the inside as well as the outside of your triorama to create your project.

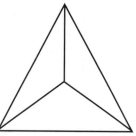

Main Assignment • Triorama, Part 2

Here are the steps for designing your triorama:

- From your study sheets, choose a biome and then choose two landforms and two bodies of water that are appropriate for your biome.

- Research any other materials that will help you better create your triorama, such as books, CD-ROMs, Internet resources, atlases, or videos.

- Make a sketch of how your triorama will look. Make a list of the materials you will need and ask your teacher if the materials are available in the classroom or if you will need to get some items from home.

- Label all of the parts of your triorama with their correct geographic terms.

- Fill in the Graphic Organizer, explaining each term clearly, with correct spelling. Display the Graphic Organizer with the finished triorama.

- Finally, on a four-inch-by-six-inch index card write a plan for:
    - How you will get to this place
    - Clothing you will need there
    - Recreational equipment you will need
    - Any other items that would be good to take on a trip to this biome

- Be sure to use correct punctuation, capitalization, and spelling when writing your plan.

- The final product should be neat and attractive, give accurate information, and be interesting to your audience.

Main Assignment • Triorama Rubric

Name   **Date**

Project Title   **Total**

Circle the number of the paragraph that best describes the student's performance on a continuum of 4 (highest) to 1 (lowest).

	4	3	2	1
Evidence of Research	The triorama includes three categories: a biome with two landforms and two bodies of water appropriate for that biome. Geographic terms are correctly explained on the graphic organizer that is displayed with the attractive triorama.	The triorama includes three categories: a biome with two landforms and two bodies of water appropriate for that biome. Most geographic terms are explained on the graphic organizer that is displayed with the triorama.	The triorama includes three categories. Though there is a biome, there is only one landform and/or one body of water displayed that are appropriate for that biome. Geographic terms are not all explained correctly on the graphic organizer that is displayed with the triorama.	There may be two or three categories represented in the presentation, and these are not necessarily appropriate for the biome. Geographic terms are missing or incorrectly explained.
Travel Plan	There is a well-defined travel plan for visiting the area, which includes appropriate items to take along and the procedure for how to get there.	There is a travel plan for visiting the area that includes appropriate items to take along and the procedure for how to get there.	The travel plan has some required information but is incomplete.	There is a minimal travel plan or none at all. The display is not well constructed and may or may not be in triorama form.
Mechanics	The plan uses correct punctuation, capitalization, and spelling.	The plan may have minor errors in punctuation, capitalization, or spelling.	There are errors in punctuation, capitalization, or spelling in the plan.	Geographic labels are missing from the plan.
Design of Display	Display is well constructed, shows creativity, and has geographic parts labeled correctly. The total project is neat and attractive.	Display is well constructed with geographic parts labeled correctly. The total project is neat and attractive.	The display shows some problems with construction and/or some mistakes on geographic labels.	The project shows little effort at following the guidelines given.

 Report Guidelines

Based on the research you have done, places you have been, and information you have learned, choose a biome.

Use the Data Collector to make notes on the following aspects of your biome:

- Areas of the Earth where the biome is found

- Its climate throughout the year

- Animal life that exists there

- Types of vegetation that exist there

- Why you chose this biome

On the back of your Data Collector, make a sketch of the biome that shows these aspects. Use all of your information to write or type a three- to four-paragraph report on your favorite biome. Edit for correct capitalization, punctuation, and spelling.

Use your original sketch to make an attractive illustration to go with your report. Display your final products on a large sheet of construction paper. You can also present your report orally to the class.

2 • Biomes and Landforms of the Earth

Extension Activity • Report Rubric

Name _____ **Date** _____

Project Title _____ **Total** _____

Circle the number of the paragraph that best describes the student's performance on a continuum of 4 (highest) to 1 (lowest).

	4	**3**	**2**	**1**
Content	The five elements of the guidelines are included in the report in an extremely interesting and creative way.	All basic elements of the guidelines are included in the report in an interesting and creative way.	Some elements of the guidelines are missing from the report.	Report includes minimal information required by the guidelines.
Organization	Information is well organized and may go beyond the required number of paragraphs (three to four).	Information is well organized and presented in the required number of paragraphs (three to four).	Information shows lack of organization. Paragraphing is not clear.	There is a lack of organization and no paragraph structure.
Mechanics	There is correct usage in sentence structure, grammar, and punctuation marks. Spelling and capitalization are used correctly.	There is correct usage in sentence structure and grammar. Capitalization, punctuation marks, and spelling errors are minor.	Simple sentence structure is present with errors in grammar. There are many capitalization, punctuation, and spelling errors.	There are many errors in sentence structure and grammar. There are many capitalization, punctuation, and spelling errors.
Overall Appearance	Report is exceptionally neat and creatively designed to demonstrate complete understanding.	Report is word processed or neatly handwritten mounted on construction paper and includes a color picture.	There is an attempt at neatness in the written report and in producing an appropriate picture.	There is little or no attempt at neatness in the written report or in producing an appropriate picture.

2 • Biomes and Landforms of the Earth

Game Show Guidelines

Games are a fun way to review and test what we know. It is also a challenge to devise a game that it is fair, interesting, and enjoyable to play.

Following are two suggestions for games that can be played using what you have learned about biomes, landforms, and bodies of water.

Question and Answer

This game is for three or more people. At least two contestants play the game and another person acts as the leader, or emcee. In each play of the game, the emcee asks a question or gives an answer, and a contestant responds with the appropriate answer or question. For example:

> *Emcee:* "The place where a river begins."
> *Contestant:* "What is the source?"
> or
> *Emcee:* "What is the source?"
> *Contestant:* "The place where a river begins."

The emcee can also use a fill-in-the-blank or complete-the-sentence format. If the contestant gives the correct response, he or she gets a point. The information in this unit offers three categories of questions: biomes, landforms, and bodies of water. Before playing, you must also make the following decisions about how to play your game:

- Length of the game
- Number of contestants
- Number of items for each category
- Number of points per answer
- How to set up the game (such as writing statements on cards to read)

Spin and Win

This game is played by two or more contestants and a leader, or emcee. The game consists of a large display of individual cards, each of which has one letter. When placed in order, the letter cards spell out a word or phrase. These cards can be displayed on a wall of the classroom or on the chalkboard with the letters facing down.

The game also includes a large spinner that is divided into segments. (You can make a spinner from poster board using a paper clip to attach the arrow.) Each segment of the spinner includes a number of points or "lose a turn." Contestants spin the spinner to find out the number of points they will receive if they guess a letter correctly, then guess a letter. If a contestant guesses a letter correctly, the emcee turns over all cards with that letter.

If a contestant lands on "lose a turn," the play moves to the next contestant. The contestant with the most points at the end of the game wins.

You can play the game with dice instead of a spinner.

Other decisions to be made for this game are:

- Length of the game
- Number of contestants
- Phrases or words to be used on the cards
- If hints will be allowed, which hints will be given

Have a good time and show what you know!

"My Favorite Place" Poem Guidelines

Following is a set of prompts for assisting a writer in creating poetry. You can read these aloud to your students, or they can use the guidelines independently. Students are to put their thoughts on paper in phrases rather than in complete sentences. They can draw pictures to illustrate the poem.

Steps to writing a "My Favorite Place" poem

- Write about your favorite place, using two or three geographic terms to describe it.

- Write about your favorite kind of day at this place, using one or two adjectives that describe the area accurately.

- Write about your favorite time of day or night at this place using two or three words.

- Close your eyes and think about two or three favorite sounds you would hear in this place. Write these down.

- Close your eyes and picture two or three favorite things that you would see in this place. Write these down.

- Write two or three favorite things you would like to do at this place.

- Write about a time that you would want to travel to this place.

- Use two or three words that tell how you would feel if you visited this place.

2 • Biomes and Landforms of the Earth

Group Evaluation

Name _____ **Date** _____

Group Name _____ **Total** _____

Fill in the blank next to each statement below with the following numbers: 4, 3, 2, or 1. Use the numbers to indicate how well the group worked together.

> **4** Very best efforts were given each time we met.
> **3** Good effort was given each time we met.
> **2** Some effort was shown, but direction was needed from outside the group.
> **1** Little effort was given to the project.

Group Members:

_____ Showed positive behavior.

_____ Cooperated by listening to each other.

_____ Shared creative ideas.

_____ Used good organizational skills.

_____ Contributed good research to develop the project.

_____ Brought and/or shared materials when needed.

_____ Cleaned up materials at the end of each work session.

_____ Produced an attractive, neat, and accurate project.

_____ Planned the presentation together, with all members taking part.

Please add any comments about the cooperative behavior of your group that you feel would be helpful for your teacher to know.

_____

_____

_____

_____

Reflection Form

Name _____ Date _____

I enjoyed learning about . . .

_____

_____

_____

I especially enjoyed doing . . .

_____

_____

_____

I am still wondering about . . .

_____

_____

_____

The materials in which I found the most information were . . .

_____

_____

_____

What I found most challenging was . . .

_____

_____

_____

I improved the most in . . .

_____

_____

_____

3 • Endangered Animals

Memo to the Teacher

Students will study endangered animals and research the reasons why they are endangered. At the end of their research, students will create a picture book about an endangered animal. This can be an independent or small-group activity.

After reviewing a student book, complete the rubric provided by circling the choice that applies to each student's or group's work. Once the project is completed, meet with the student or group to share the completed rubric to help students understand how to improve their next presentation.

If students worked on a project in a cooperative group, they should complete the Group Evaluation together. This evaluation offers students the opportunity to assess the effectiveness of their group by focusing on what worked and what might need improvement. Students are to fill out the forms and share their responses as a group.

At the end of the unit, the students will fill out a Reflection Form to encourage individual learners to think about how and what they have learned. Students write their responses to the questions to share with the class. File evaluations for use during parent conferences.

After students finish the main assignment, you may add to, delete, or require one or more of the extension activities as part of the unit. Many of the extensions include assessment rubrics.

★ Unit Goals

Content Objective:
Become knowledgeable about endangered species and why these animals are at risk.

Performance Objective:
Create an "Endangered Animal Picture Book," including important facts about an endangered animal.

3 • Endangered Animals

 Main Assignment

Each student or group needs one copy of each of the following handouts:

- Main Assignment and Extensions
- Graphic Organizer (3 pages)
- Data Collector (2 pages)
- Picture Book Guidelines
- Picture Book Rubric
- Group Evaluation
- Reflection Form

 Extension Activities

If students pursue additional activities, each student will need one copy of each of the following:

Create a Model from Clay or Papier-mâché
- Endangered Animal Model Guidelines

Design an Illustrated Calendar
- Illustrated Calendar Guidelines
- Blank Calendar Form (12 per student)
- Calendar Rubric

Create an Endangered Animal T-shirt with an Image and a Slogan
- T-shirt Guidelines

 Internet Resources

Endangered or Extinct Critters:
   http://www.kidsdomain.com/kids/links/Endangered_or_Extinct_Critters.html

Earth's Endangered Creatures:
   http://www.endangeredcreatures.net

Student Projects

 Main Assignment

Collect data about an endangered animal. Why has this animal become endangered?

When you have finished your research, use the information you have found to create a picture book about the animal.

Extension Activities

After you complete the main assignment, show what you have learned by completing one of the following extension activities. Your teacher will provide information about each activity and ask you to work independently, in a small group, or with the whole class.

1. Create a model of an endangered animal from clay, papier-mâché, or other materials of your choice.

2. Design a calendar with the image of an endangered animal. Also include interesting facts about the animal.

3. Create a T-shirt with a picture of an endangered animal and a catchy slogan.

4. Other Activity: _____

3 • Endangered Animals

Name _____   Date _____

Habitat	Geographical location

Endangered animal

Diet	Enemies

Graphic Organizer, Part 2

Name _____ **Date** _____

Reason(s) animal is endangered

What is being done to help the animal survive?

Name _____ **Date** _____

3 • Endangered Animals

Endangered Animal Source List

List your references. Include authors and titles.

_____

_____

_____

_____

_____

_____

_____

_____

_____

_____

_____

_____

_____

_____

_____

_____

_____

_____

_____

_____

_____

_____

_____

Data Collector, Part 1

3 • Endangered Animals

Name _____ **Date** _____

Name of the endangered animal:

_____

What type of animal is it?

_____

_____

Describe the animal's natural habitat.

_____

_____

_____

_____

In what geographic regions can the animal be found?

_____

_____

_____

_____

Endangered animal's diet:

_____

_____

_____

_____

Who or what are the animal's enemies?

_____

_____

_____

_____

Data Collector, Part 2

Name _____ **Date** _____

How does the animal defend itself?

_____

_____

_____

_____

Why is this animal endangered?

_____

_____

_____

_____

What is being done to help this animal survive?

_____

_____

_____

_____

Write two or three interesting facts about the animal.

_____

_____

_____

_____

Why did you choose this animal?

_____

_____

_____

_____

On a separate sheet of paper, draw a picture of the animal in its natural habitat.

Main Assignment • Picture Book

Picture Book Guidelines

Use the information from your Graphic Organizer and Data Collector to create a picture book about your endangered animal.

Follow these guidelines:

- Your picture book should include a cover, title page, and at least 10 to 15 pages.

- The book should contain text and illustrations that depict the following information about the animal:
  - Diet
  - Habitat
  - Geographical location
  - Enemies
  - Means of defense
  - Why the animal is endangered
  - What is being done to help the endangered animal
  - Interesting facts about the animal

- The text should demonstrate your knowledge of the topic and be easily understood.

- Your illustrations should be appealing and add interest to the text.

- Edit the text for correct capitalization, punctuation, and spelling.

3 • Endangered Animals

Name _____ **Date** _____

Project Title _____ **Total** _____

Circle the number of the paragraph that best describes the student's performance on a continuum of 4 (highest) to 1 (lowest).

	4	3	2	1
Overall Presentation	The picture book is unique and visually appealing and shows exceptional mastery of the topic. It contains all criteria (diet, habitat, and so on) found in the guidelines.	The picture book demonstrates mastery of the topic. It is organized and easy to understand.	The picture book demonstrates limited mastery of the topic. It is unorganized and difficult to follow.	The book shows little or no understanding of the topic. It is visually unappealing and difficult to comprehend.
Mechanics	The text uses correct writing conventions (mechanics, spelling, and so on).	There are only minor text errors in mechanics and grammar.	Poor writing skills are evident, including misspelled words.	Numerous errors are evident.
Content	The number of pages meets or exceeds the criteria. The text is expressive and informative.	The picture book guideline criteria are evident and expressed in an easily understood manner.	Most of the criteria found in the guidelines are evident, but the book is poorly organized and difficult to comprehend.	The picture book shows student has little or no understanding of endangered animals and is difficult to follow.
Illustrations	Illustrations show high level of understanding of the topic and concepts. Exceptional use of detail and organization is evident.	Illustrations show good understanding of endangered animals and their plight. They are visually appealing and expressive.	Illustrations show some knowledge of endangered animals.	Illustrations show little or no understanding of endangered animals. They are unattractive and difficult to follow.

Endangered Animal Model Guidelines

Use the information from your Graphic Organizer and Data Collector to create a model of your endangered animal.

Follow these guidelines:

- Use clay, papier-mâché, or other materials of your choice for your model.

- The model should show the animal in its natural habitat.

- Make sure your model is realistic. Use other materials, such as fabric or pipe cleaners, to enhance the animal and its habitat.

- Your model should have a 3-inch-by-5-inch index card that includes the name of the endangered animal and a brief summary of important facts about it.

3 • Endangered Animals

3 • Endangered Animals

 ## Illustrated Calendar Guidelines

After researching an endangered animal, use the information from your Graphic Organizer and Data Collector to help you create an interesting 12-month calendar that showcases the endangered animal.

Your calendar should include the following:

• A picture and an interesting fact about the endangered animal for each month.

• Facts and one or more pictures about the endangered animal's:
  –natural habitat
  –eating habits
  –enemies
  –geographic location (habitat)
  –reason it is endangered
  –actions being taken to save it

• Use the blank calendar form provided by your teacher or create your own using art supplies or a computer program.

• Include the following details on your form:

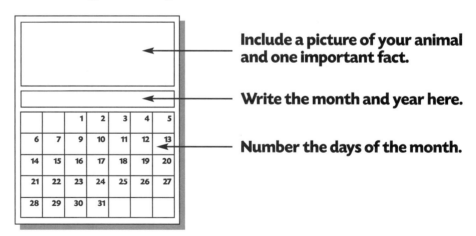

Include a picture of your animal and one important fact.

Write the month and year here.

Number the days of the month.

• You can create the illustrations by hand, use a computer drawing program, or use computer clip art.

• The calendar should be neat, colorful, and attractive.

• Check for correct capitalization, punctuation, and spelling.

Extension Activity • Calendar Rubric

Name _____ **Date** _____

Project Title _____ **Total** _____

Circle the number of the paragraph that best describes the student's performance on a continuum of 4 (highest) to 1 (lowest).

	4	**3**	**2**	**1**
Overall Presentation	The calendar shows a high level of creativity and knowledge about the animal. The calendar illustrates the endangered animal topic.	The calendar is creative and interesting. Style and design are evident. The calendar represents the topic.	The calendar demonstrates limited creativity and knowledge. The calendar attempts to represent some aspect of the topic.	The calendar shows lack of creativity and has little appeal.
Content	The calendar demonstrates a high level of knowledge about the animal.	The calendar demonstrates mastery of the topic.	The calendar demonstrates limited understanding of the endangered animal.	The calendar demonstrates little or no understanding of the topic.
Guideline Criteria	The calendar includes all guideline criteria in a unique manner.	The calendar contains detailed facts and illustrations.	The calendar contains few details about the animal and only some of the guideline criteria.	The calendar is not informative and is inaccurate.
Calendar Design and Illustrations	The illustrations reflect understanding and high level of knowledge about the animal. They are extremely appealing and attractive.	The illustrations and overall design are appealing and interesting.	The illustrations attempt to appeal and interest readers.	The illustrations are messy and unattractive and do not complement the facts.

 T-shirt Guidelines

After researching an endangered animal, design and create a T-shirt that showcases your animal. The materials you will need and some tips to help you create your T-shirt follows.

Materials:

Pre-washed, light-colored T-shirt

Large piece of cardboard that will fit inside the T-shirt

Fabric markers

Fabric paints

T-shirt Instructions:

- Before beginning, make a few preliminary sketches of the endangered animal.

- Decide if you want to include the animal's habitat on the T-shirt.

- Invent a slogan or message about saving and/or protecting the endangered animal.

- Place the large piece of cardboard inside the pre-washed T-shirt to prevent the marker or paints from bleeding through to the back of the shirt.

- Use the fabric marker to sketch the animal.

- Fill in the sketch with fabric paints.

- Let the paints dry thoroughly before wearing the shirt.

- Wear your T-shirt to class on the designated date.

3 • Endangered Animals

Group Evaluation

Name _____   **Date** _____

Group Name (s) _____   **Total** _____

Fill in the blank next to each statement below with the following numbers: 4, 3, 2, or 1. Use the numbers to indicate how well the group worked together.

> **4** Very best efforts were given each time we met.
> **3** Good effort was given each time we met.
> **2** Some effort was shown, but direction was needed from outside the group.
> **1** Little effort was given to the project.

Group Members:

_____ Showed positive behavior.

_____ Cooperated by listening to each other.

_____ Shared creative ideas.

_____ Used good organizational skills.

_____ Contributed good research to develop the project.

_____ Brought and/or shared materials when needed.

_____ Cleaned up materials at the end of each work session.

_____ Produced an attractive, neat, and accurate project.

_____ Planned the presentation together, with all members taking part.

Please add any comments about the cooperative behavior of your group that you feel would be helpful for your teacher to know.

_____

_____

_____

_____

Reflection Form

3 • Endangered Animals

Name _____ Date _____

I enjoyed learning about . . .
_____
_____
_____

I especially enjoyed doing . . .
_____
_____
_____

I am still wondering about . . .
_____
_____
_____

The materials in which I found the most information were . . .
_____
_____
_____

What I found most challenging was . . .
_____
_____
_____

I improved the most in . . .
_____
_____
_____

4 • Insects and Arachnids

Memo to the Teacher

This unit gives students an opportunity to research the characteristics of insects and arachnids. At the end of their research, students will create a Venn diagram poster.

Students will show their knowledge by displaying information and images related to how insects and arachnids are alike or different. Students can create the poster independently if they choose to research both insects and arachnids, or they can interview a partner and share information. (Because this is a project of comparing and contrasting, it is more conducive to the pairing and sharing strategy.)

After reviewing the posters, complete the rubric provided for each student or each member of a pair by circling the number of the paragraph that applies to that student's work. Then meet with students to share the rubric.

If students worked on a project in a cooperative group, they should complete the Group Evaluation together. This evaluation offers students the opportunity to assess the effectiveness of their group or partnership by focusing on what worked and what might need improvement. Students fill out the Group Evaluation and share their responses.

At the end of the unit, the students will fill out a Reflection Form to encourage individual learners to think about how and what they have learned. Students write their responses to the questions and share their responses with the class. File evaluations for use during parent conferences.

Following the main assignment, you may add to, delete, or require one or more of the extension activities as part of the unit. Many of the extensions include assessment rubrics.

★ Unit Goals

Content Objective:
Become knowledgeable about the similarities and differences between insects and arachnids.

Performance Objective:
Visually demonstrate an understanding of the comparison of the two species, using a Venn diagram.

Materials and Resources

Main Assignment

Each student or group needs one copy of each of the following handouts:

- Main Assignment
- Graphic Organizer (2 pages)
- Data Collector (2 pages)
- Venn Diagram Poster Guidelines
- Venn Diagram
- Report Guidelines
- Venn Diagram Rubric
- Group Evaluation
- Reflection Form

Extension Activities

If students pursue additional activities, each student will need one copy of each of the following:

Write Cinquain Poetry
- Cinquain Poem Guidelines

*Conduct an Interview Based on Chris van Allsburg's **Two Bad Ants***
- Interview Guidelines
- Interview Rubric

Create a "Bug Home" Model
- Model Home Guidelines
- "Bug Home" Model Rubric

Internet Resources

Bugbios: http://www.bugbios.com

Alien Empire: http: www.pbs.org/wnet/naturalalienempire

Class Insecta: http://www.insecta.com/insecta/index.shtml

Learning About Arachnids:
   http://wildnetafrica.co.za/wildlifestuff/juniorpage/scorpions/scorpion.html

Student Projects

Main Assignment

Research and collect data about insects and/or arachnids. Use the Graphic Organizer to collect your data. The Data Collector will help you develop more detailed information from your notes and organize it into complete sentences. When you have finished your research, use the information you have found to create a poster that compares and contrasts, in text and in pictures, insects and arachnids.

Extension Activities

After you complete the main assignment, show what you have learned by completing one of the following extension activities. Your teacher will provide more information about each activity and ask you to work independently, in a small group, or with the whole class.

1. Write two cinquain poems (five lines in each). One poem will be about an insect, and one poem will be about an arachnid.

2. Read the book, *Two Bad Ants* by Chris van Allsburg. Think of questions about the story and interview another student. The other student will answer the questions from one of the ant's point of view.

3. Create a model of a "Bug Condo" or a "Spider Townhouse."

4. Other Activity: _____

Name _____ **Date** _____

4 • Insects and Arachnids

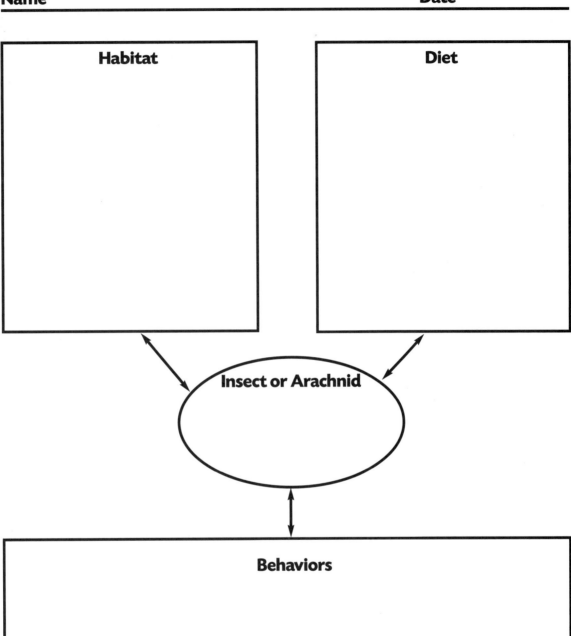

| Habitat | Diet |

Insect or Arachnid

Behaviors

Name _____ **Date** _____

4 • Insects and Arachnids

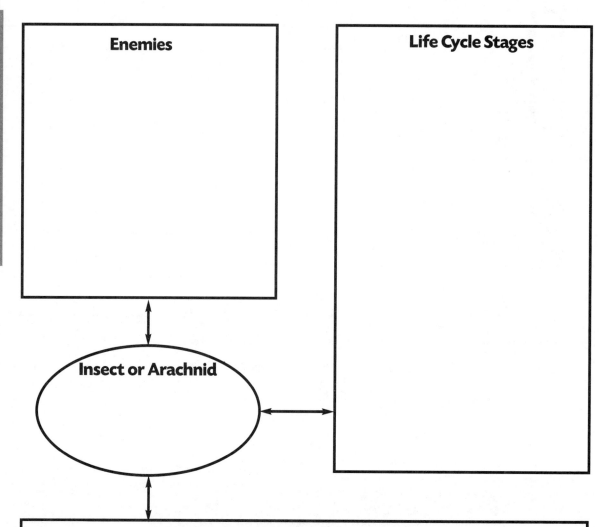

Enemies

Life Cycle Stages

Insect or Arachnid

Physical Characteristics of Adult Stage

Data Collector, Part 1

4 • Insects and Arachnids

Name _____ **Date** _____

Name of the insect or arachnid:

_____

What are the stages of the creature's life cycle?

_____
_____
_____
_____
_____
_____

Describe the physical characteristics of the creature's adult stage (color, size, and body parts).

_____
_____
_____
_____
_____
_____

Describe your creature's habitat.

_____
_____
_____
_____
_____

Name _____ **Date** _____

4 • Insects and Arachnids

What does your creature eat?

_____

_____

_____

_____

_____

_____

Name this creature's enemies.

_____

_____

_____

_____

_____

_____

_____

Describe your creature's behavior. Is your creature helpful and/or harmful to certain environments, humans, and other creatures?

_____

_____

_____

_____

_____

_____

_____

_____

_____

_____

Sketch and label the adult creature on the back of this page.

4 • Insects and Arachnids

Venn Diagram Poster Guidelines

After collecting data on an insect and/or arachnid, use your information to develop a poster designed to compare and contrast your creatures.

1. Use a piece of poster board or butcher paper that is approximately 24 by 36 inches. Following is one suggestion for how to arrange information in mini-Venn diagrams:

Title of Poster	
I	II
III	IV

2. Put a title at the top of your poster. Your teacher will provide four blank Venn diagrams. Carefully label and illustrate each diagram. Then, using words and images, compare and contrast your insects and arachnids in the following categories:

Section I: Life cycle stages
Section II: Colors, sizes, and body structures in the adult stages
Section III: Habitats, diets, and enemies
Section IV: Ways in which they are helpful and/or harmful (to nature, humans, and other creatures)

Use cutouts, drawings, or computer-generated illustrations on your poster.

3. The final copy must be word processed or neatly handwritten. Edit for correct capitalization, punctuation, and spelling.

4. Include a Bibliography page (see Report Guidelines), Graphic Organizer, and Data Collector.

Name _____ **Date** _____

4 • Insects and Arachnids

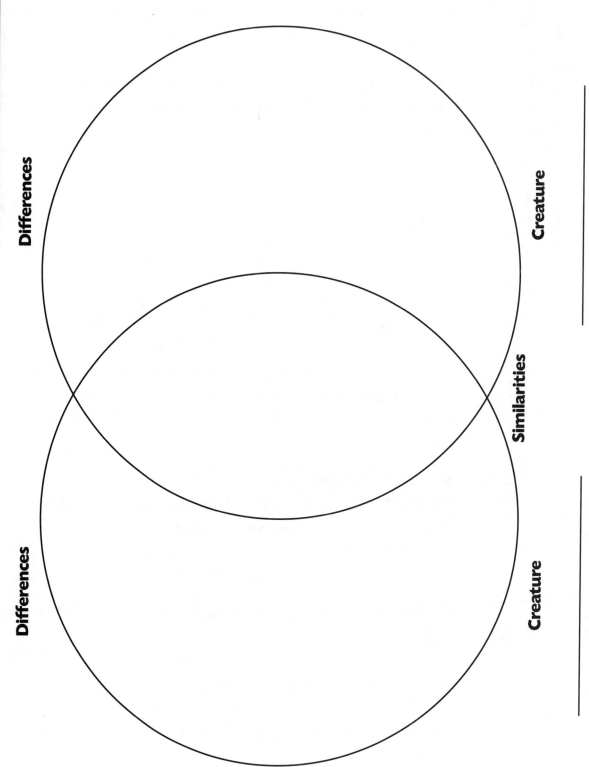

Differences

Creature

Similarities

Differences

Creature

Main Assignment • Venn Diagram Rubric

Name _____ **Date** _____

Project Title _____ **Total** _____

Circle the number of the paragraph that best describes the student's performance on a continuum of 4 (highest) to 1 (lowest).

	4	3	2	1
Overall Presentation	Poster is visually appealing and well organized. Text is neat and correctly written.	Poster is well organized and easily understood. Text is neat with a few minor errors.	Poster shows that there has been an attempt to organize information, but it is not easily understood. Text shows a number of errors.	Poster shows that there has been little or no attempt to organize information, as stated in the guidelines. It is hard to understand and has many errors.
Bibliography	Poster is properly identified with a complete bibliography in correct form.	Poster is properly identified with a bibliography in correct form.	Poster identification and bibliography are included, not necessarily in correct form.	Poster identification and bibliography may or may not be present.
Evidence of Research	Poster shows student has an exceptional mastery of topics. It follows the guidelines and correctly compares and contrasts two creatures throughout the four sections.	Poster shows student has a mastery of topics. It follows the guidelines and correctly compares and contrasts two creatures throughout the four sections.	Poster shows student has made an attempt to compare and contrast two creatures throughout the four sections. Some information may be missing.	Poster shows student has made little or no attempt to compare and contrast creatures throughout the four sections.
Illustrations	Originality is apparent. Illustrations are visually appealing and enhance information throughout the four sections in a creative way.	Illustrations complement information throughout the four sections.	Illustrations are used throughout the four sections but do not enhance information.	There are few or no illustrations relating to the information.

4 • Insects and Arachnids

✏ Cinquain Poetry Guidelines

A cinquain is a form of poetry that uses five lines to tell about someone or something in nature. As shown in the example, the "thing" you are describing can change as you add ideas to the poem.

Line 1: One noun or proper noun (could be life cycle stage name)

Line 2: Two adjectives

Line 3: Three verbs ending in *-ing*

Line 4: A sentence or phrase about the word in line 1.

Line 5: A synonym for or description of the first word.

Title your poem.

Example:

"Caterpillar into Butterfly"

Caterpillar

Fuzzy, crawly

Squirming, growing, spinning

I'm going to be beautiful in the spring!

Butterfly

4 • Insects and Arachnids

 ## Interview Guidelines

With your partner, read *Two Bad Ants* by author Chris van Allsburg. Make a list of interview questions and prepare the answers from an ant's point of view about the ants' adventures in the book. Use these questions and answers to conduct an interview with your partner about the book. One person will be the interviewer who asks the questions, and the other person will be interviewed as if he or she were one of the ants in the story.

Following are guidelines for your interview/oral presentation:

- Be sure to ask questions that show your knowledge of real ants and of the fictional ants in the book. Use the notes on insects and arachnids from your Graphic Organizers or your Data Collectors.

  Here are a few sample questions:
    Why did you go to that house?
    What path did you take to get there?
    How did you feel when you were left behind?

- Decide who will be the interviewer and who will answer the questions. Practice your interview.

- Speak loudly, clearly, and with expression.

- Have fun, and your audience will, too.

Extension Activity • Interview Rubric

Name _____ **Date** _____

Project Title _____ **Total** _____

Circle the number of the paragraph that best describes the student's performance on a continuum of 4 (highest) to 1 (lowest).

	4	3	2	1
Overall Presentation	Interview presentation demonstrates a high level mastery of the topic. There is a high degree of understanding and insight.	Interview presentation shows knowledge of the topic. There is apparent understanding and insight.	Interview presentation shows limited knowledge of the topic. Some confusion is apparent.	Presentation shows little or no understanding of the topic.
Content	Interview is unique and presents information in an original way.	Interview is creative, interesting, and informative.	An attempt has been made to make the interview presentation interesting.	Interview form is not present and there is a lack of creativity.
Style	Interview demonstrates a keen sense of drama and timing.	Interview shows effective drama and timing.	Interview shows limited understanding of drama and timing.	Presentation shows no drama or timing.
Delivery	Presenters speak loudly, clearly, and with expression.	Presenters are easily heard and understood.	Presenters are not easily heard and use little expression.	Presenters are unable to be heard or understood.

4 • Insects and Arachnids

 ## Model Home Guidelines

Using your knowledge of the kind of habitat required by insects and arachnids, design a "Bug Condo" or a "Spider Townhouse." Let your imagination run wild!

- Draw a floor plan and label each room. Include plenty of rooms in your floor plan to meet the needs of your creature. This will be the plan for your model.

- Gather building materials such as glue, scissors, small boxes or cardboard, colored construction paper, twigs, string, and so on.

- Create your model according to the floor plan. Place a small card in each room to explain how the home meets your creature's needs. Use notes from your Graphic Organizer, Data Collector, or Venn diagram.

- When completed, display the model home for everyone to view.

Extension Activity • Model Home Rubric

Name _____ **Date** _____

Project Title _____ **Total** _____

Circle the number of the paragraph that best describes the student's performance on a continuum of 4 (highest) to 1 (lowest).

	4	**3**	**2**	**1**
Content	Model shows a high level mastery of the topic by the cards of information placed in each room.	Model shows good mastery of the topic by the cards of information placed in each room.	Model shows limited mastery of the topic based on the information cards used.	Model shows little or no mastery of the topic. Information cards are missing.
Overall Presentation	Model is unique and highly creative.	Model has thoughtful design.	Student has made some attempt at design.	Student has made little or no attempt at design.
Construction	The model is well built, attractive, and easy to view.	The model is well built, attractive, and easy to view.	The model is weakly built.	The model lacks sturdiness and neatness.
Use of Materials	Exceptional attention has been given to detail, color, and the variety of materials used.	There is good use of color, and a variety of materials have been used.	There is some variety in the use of color and materials.	There is little variety in the use of color and materials.

Group Evaluation

Name _____ **Date** _____

Group Name (s) _____ **Total** _____

Fill in the blank next to each statement below with the following numbers: 4, 3, 2, or 1. Use the numbers to tell your teacher how the group worked together.

> **4** Very best efforts were given each time we met.
> **3** Good effort was given each time we met.
> **2** Some effort was shown, but direction was needed from outside the group.
> **1** Little effort was given to the project.

Group Members:

_____ Showed positive behavior.

_____ Cooperated by listening to each other.

_____ Shared creative ideas.

_____ Used good organizational skills.

_____ Contributed good research to develop the project.

_____ Brought and/or shared materials when needed.

_____ Cleaned up materials at the end of each work session.

_____ Produced an attractive, neat, and accurate project.

_____ Planned the presentation together, with all members taking part.

Please add any comments about the cooperative behavior of your group that you feel would be helpful for your teacher to know.

_____

_____

_____

_____

Reflection Form

Name _____ **Date** _____

I enjoyed learning about . . .
_____
_____
_____

I especially enjoyed doing . . .
_____
_____
_____

I am still wondering about . . .
_____
_____
_____

The materials in which I found the most information were . . .
_____
_____
_____

What I found most challenging was . . .
_____
_____
_____

I improved the most in . . .
_____
_____
_____

5 • Inventors and Inventions

Memo to the Teacher

Students will choose one invention that interests them and research the invention and its inventor. At the end of their research, students will design and write a fact-based newspaper, complete with illustrations and advertisements. Students will use both a Graphic Organizer and a Data Collector in writing their newspapers. This can be an independent or a small-group activity.

After reviewing a student newspaper, complete the rubric provided by circling the number of the paragraph that applies to each student's or group's work. After the project is completed, share the rubric with the student or group to help students improve their next project.

If students worked on a project in a cooperative group, they should complete the Group Evaluation together. This evaluation offers students the opportunity to assess the effectiveness of their group by focusing on what worked and what might need improvement. Students are to fill out the form and share their responses.

At the end of the unit, the students will fill out a Reflection Form to encourage individual learners to think about how and what they have learned. Students write their responses to the questions to share with the class. File evaluations for use during parent conferences.

After students finish the main assignment, you may add to, delete, or require one or more of the extension activities. Many of the extensions include assessment rubrics.

★ Unit Goals

Content Objective:
Learn about the impact of inventions on the world and about the inventors who created them.

Performance Objective:
Work in a cooperative group to create a fact-based newspaper about inventions and inventors.

Materials and Resources

Main Assignment

Each student or group needs one copy of each of the following handouts:

- Main Assignment
- Graphic Organizer (2 pages)
- Data Collector (2 pages)
- Questions About Inventors
- Newspaper Guidelines
- Newspaper Layout, Page 1
- Newspaper Layout, Page 2
- Newspaper Rubric
- Group Evaluation
- Reflection Form

✏ Extension Activities

If students pursue additional activities, each student will need one copy of each of the following:

Create an Invention Time Line
- Time Line Guidelines

Make an Oral Presentation about an Inventor and Invention
- Oral Presentation Guidelines
- Oral Presentation Rubric

Design a Venn Diagram Poster Comparing and Contrasting Inventors and Inventions
- Venn Diagram Poster Guidelines
- Blank Venn Diagram
- Venn Diagram Poster Rubric

🖥 Internet Resources

Inventions and Inventors:
> http://www.enchantedlearning.com/inventors/

The Greatest Inventors and Inventions (Jr. ThinkQuest site):
> http:// tqjunior.thinkquest.org/5847/

Inventors Museum Online:
> http://www.inventorsmuseum.com/museum_map.htm

Student Projects

Main Assignment

Choose a famous invention and collect the following data about the invention and its inventor:

- Describe the invention and state the year it was invented.

- Research the life of the inventor.

- What was unique, if anything, about the person who created this invention?

- What events were happening in the world at the time the invention was made?

- Describe the need for such an invention at this time in history.

- How has this invention had an impact on human beings and our world?

When you have finished your research, write and design a newspaper filled with information about your inventor and invention.

Extension Activities

After you complete the main assignment, show what you have learned by completing one of the following extension activities. Your teacher will provide more information about each activity and ask you to work independently, in a small group, or with the whole class.

1. Create a time line of at least 15 inventions that have been researched by you and your classmates.

2. Make an oral presentation about your inventor and invention.

3. Design a Venn diagram poster that compares and contrasts your inventor and one other inventor and his or her invention.

4. Other Activity: _____

5 • Inventors and Inventions

Name _____   Date _____

Date and place of birth	Where inventor lived

Inventor

Interests and education	Important facts

Recognized accomplishments

5 • Inventors and Inventions

Name _____

Date _____

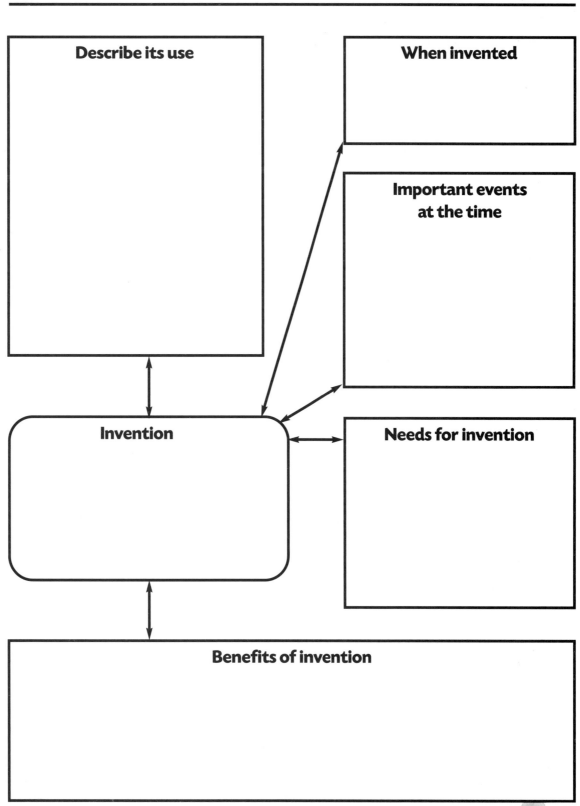

Describe its use

When invented

Important events at the time

Invention

Needs for invention

Benefits of invention

Data Collector, Part 1

Name _____ **Date** _____

Name of the invention:

_____

Inventor's name:

_____

Write a brief summary of the inventor's life, including birth and death dates, where he or she was born, and other important facts about this inventor.

_____

_____

_____

_____

_____

_____

_____

_____

_____

_____

_____

Write two interesting facts about the inventor not mentioned above.

1. _____

_____

_____

2. _____

_____

_____

In what year was the invention made?

_____

Data Collector, Part 2

5 • Inventors and Inventions

Name _____ **Date** _____

List two important world events that occurred during the year in which the invention was invented.

1. _____

_____

2. _____

_____

How did the invention benefit people?

_____

_____

_____

_____

_____

Describe how the invention works.

_____

_____

_____

_____

_____

List the titles and authors of references.

_____

_____

_____

_____

_____

_____

Sketch the invention on drawing paper.

Questions About Inventors

After researching and writing a biographical profile of an inventor, choose two of the following questions to answer and include in your newspaper.

1. What hardships did your inventor face? How did he or she resolve or overcome these difficulties?

2. Name two major world events that happened about the time the invention was created. Describe the social, economic, and political environment of that time in history.

3. Talk to another researcher and compare and contrast the lives of two inventors.

4. What is creativity? Can it be taught? Explain your answers.

5. Does competition foster or inhibit creative thinking? Why? Give a detailed explanation based on the life of the inventor you researched.

6. What are the urgent problems of today that require creative minds?

7. How are creative men and women like or not like other people?

Newspaper Guidelines

Write and design a newspaper filled with information about your inventor and invention. Following are guidelines to use in writing the articles for your newspaper:

- Give your newspaper a creative title that relates to inventions and choose a publication date late in the inventor's lifetime. Articles, pictures, and advertisements should relate to this time in history.

- Include at least three articles about an invention and its inventor that address who, what, when, where, and how. These articles might be about a particular invention, what events or needs led to its invention, the life of the inventor, and ways in which the invention helped or changed society.

- Give each article a headline that introduces the text.

- Use pictures, photographs, cartoons, or comic strips to illustrate your newspaper. All illustrations should be appealing and relevant to the topic.

- Include one to three advertisements for goods or services appropriate to the time in history.

- The final copy of the newspaper is to be word processed or hand written using a newspaper-like format and should contain correct sentence structure, spelling, capitalization, and punctuation.

5 • Inventors and Inventions

Name _____ **Date** _____

Title of the Newspaper
_____

Headline	**Headline**
_____	_____
_____	_____

Article
_____
_____
_____
_____
_____
_____

Article
_____
_____
_____
_____
_____
_____

Headline
_____
_____

Advertisement
_____
_____
_____
_____
_____

Article
_____
_____
_____
_____
_____
_____

5 • Inventors and Inventions

Name _____ **Date** _____

Comic Strip or Illustrations

Headline
_____
_____

Headline
_____
_____

Article
_____
_____
_____
_____
_____
_____

Article
_____
_____
_____
_____
_____
_____

Advertisement
_____
_____
_____
_____

Advertisement
_____
_____
_____
_____

Main Assignment • Newspaper Rubric

Name _____ **Date** _____

Project Title _____ **Total** _____

Circle the number of the paragraph that best describes the student's performance on a continuum of 4 (highest) to 1 (lowest).

	4	3	2	1
Overall Presentation	The newspaper is unique and visually appealing and shows exceptional mastery of the topic.	The newspaper demonstrates mastery of the topic.	The newspaper demonstrates limited mastery of the topic.	The newspaper shows little or no understanding of the topic.
Mechanics	The text follows correct writing guidelines (mechanics, spelling, and so on).	Text is organized and easy to understand. There are minor text errors (spelling, mechanics, and so on).	Poor writing skills are evident, including misspelled words. It is unorganized and difficult to follow.	Text is visually unappealing and difficult to comprehend. Numerous errors are evident.
Content	The newspaper contains all the criteria listed in the guidelines in a manner that exhibits superior knowledge of the topic.	Guideline criteria are evident and content is expressed in an easily understood manner.	Most of the guideline criteria are evident, but text is poorly organized and difficult to comprehend.	The newspaper shows student has little or no understanding of the topic, and text is difficult to follow.
Comic Strips/ Illustrations	Comic strips and/or illustrations show a high level of understanding of the topic and concepts. Exceptional use of detail, layout, and organization are evident.	Comic strips and/or illustrations show good understanding of the topic and concepts. They are visually appealing and expressive.	Comic strips and/or illustrations show some knowledge of the topic and concepts. The pictures are neat and somewhat attractive.	Comic strips and/or illustrations show little or no understanding of the topic. They are visually unappealing and do nothing to enhance the topic.

 Time Line Guidelines

After you have finished researching inventions and inventors, interview classmates to collect data for an Invention Time Line. Add their data to this time line to develop a look at inventions over a period of time.

Follow these guidelines to create your Inventions Time Line:

- The time line should contain at least fifteen inventions.

- List the inventions in chronological order.

- Show a date and illustration for each invention.

- Illustrations should be hand-drawn.

5 • Inventors and Inventions

Oral Presentation Guidelines
Be the Inventor!

After researching your inventor and his or her invention, develop an oral presentation based on the information you have found.

Follow these guidelines:

• Include information that demonstrates your knowledge of the inventor and his or her most important invention.

• Be the inventor! Speak to the audience from the inventor's point of view.

• Be creative! Props or costumes are a great way to share information with your audience.

• Speak loudly, clearly, and with expression.

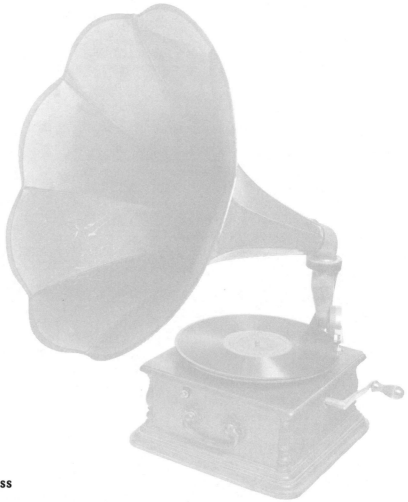

Extension Activity • Oral Presentation Rubric

Name _____ **Date** _____

Project Title _____ **Total** _____

Circle the number of the paragraph that best describes the student's performance on a continuum of 4 (highest) to 1 (lowest).

5 • Inventors and Inventions

	4	**3**	**2**	**1**
Content	Presentation demonstrates high level mastery of the topic.	Knowledge of the topic is evident.	Presentation demonstrates limited knowledge of the topic.	Presentation demonstrates little or no knowledge of the topic.
Style	Presentation reflects a high degree of understanding and insight.	Presentation is easy to follow and understand.	Presentation is difficult to follow.	Presentation lacks style and creativity.
Creativity	Presentation is unique and presents information in an original way.	Presentation is creative and interesting.	Presenter has made an attempt to make the presentation interesting.	Presenter has little or no understanding of drama and timing.
Delivery	Presentation demonstrates keen sense of drama and timing. Presenter speaks loudly, clearly, and with expression.	Presenter uses a sense of drama and timing to communicate effectively with the audience. Presenter is easily heard and understood.	Limited understanding of drama and timing are apparent. Presenter is not easily heard and uses little oral expression.	Presenter is unable to be heard or understood.

5 • Inventors and Inventions

 ## Venn Diagram Poster Guidelines

After collecting data, work with another student to create a poster that compares and contrasts your inventors and inventions. To display your work, use poster board or craft paper that measures approximately 24 inches by 36 inches.

- Your poster should contain a title, your name and your partner's name.

- The poster should compare and contrast both inventors and inventions based on your research data.

- Compare and contrast major world events that occurred during the time the inventions were introduced.

- Compare and contrast ways that the inventions have benefited mankind.

- Poster text should be word processed or written neatly with correct capitalization, punctuation, and spelling. Edit for clear understanding.

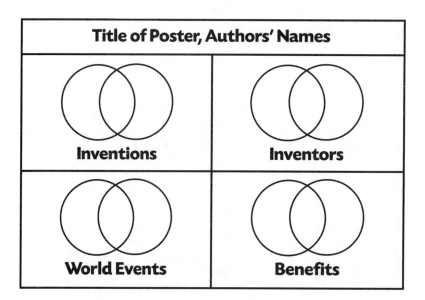

© 2002 Rigby

Name _____ **Date** _____

5 • Inventors and Inventions

Differences

Inventor/Invention

Similarities

Differences

Inventor/Invention

Extension Activity • Venn Diagram Poster Rubric

Name _____ **Date** _____

Project Title _____ **Total** _____

Circle the number of the paragraph that best describes the student's performance on a continuum of 4 (highest) to 1 (lowest).

	4	**3**	**2**	**1**
Overall Poster	Poster is visually appealing and well organized. Text is neat and correctly written.	Poster is well organized and easily understood. Text is neat with a few minor errors.	Poster shows an attempt to organize information but is not easily understood. Text has a number of errors.	Poster shows students have made little or no attempt to organize information as stated in the guidelines. Poster is hard to understand and has many errors.
Bibliography	Poster has a properly identified bibliography.	Poster includes an accurate bibliography.	Poster identification and bibliography are included but not necessarily in the correct order.	Poster identification and bibliography may or may not be present.
Content	Poster shows exceptional mastery of topics. It correctly compares and contrasts two inventors or inventions. Originality is apparent.	Poster shows mastery of topics. It correctly compares and contrasts two inventors or inventions.	Poster shows an attempt to compare and contrast the inventions or inventors. Some information may be missing.	Poster shows little or no attempt to compare and contrast inventions or inventors.
Illustrations	Illustrations are visually appealing and enhance information.	Illustrations complement information on the poster.	Illustrations are used but do not enhance the information.	There are few or no illustrations that relate to the topic.

Group Evaluation

Name _____ **Date** _____

Group Name (s) _____ **Total** _____

Fill in the blank next to each statement below with the following numbers: 4, 3, 2, or 1. Use the numbers to indicate how well the group worked together.

> **4** Very best efforts were given each time we met.
> **3** Good effort was given each time we met.
> **2** Some effort was shown, but direction was needed from outside the group.
> **1** Little effort was given to the project.

Group Members:

_____ Showed positive behavior.

_____ Cooperated by listening to each other.

_____ Shared creative ideas.

_____ Used good organizational skills.

_____ Contributed good research to develop the project.

_____ Brought and/or shared materials when needed.

_____ Cleaned up materials at the end of each work session.

_____ Produced an attractive, neat, and accurate project.

_____ Planned the presentation together, with all members taking part.

Please add any comments about the cooperative behavior of your group that you feel would be helpful for your teacher to know.

_____

_____

_____

_____

5 • Inventors and Inventions

Reflection Form

Name _____ **Date** _____

I enjoyed learning about . . .
_____
_____
_____

I especially enjoyed doing . . .
_____
_____
_____

I am still wondering about . . .
_____
_____
_____

The materials in which I found the most information were . . .
_____
_____
_____

What I found most challenging was . . .
_____
_____
_____

I improved the most in . . .
_____
_____
_____

6 • Natural Disasters

Memo to the Teacher

Students will find textbooks, trade books, encyclopedias, videos, and the Internet useful while doing research on natural disasters. They can write or call the local or national weather bureaus for information.

At the end of their research, students will design and write a video documentary that focuses on one type of natural disaster and informs the audience about the causes, historical effects, safety issues, and other information about that disaster. It is a good idea to have students approach this project in pairs or groups of three.

After viewing each video, complete the rubric provided by circling the choice in each row that applies to the group's work. After the presentation, meet with the small groups of students and share the rubric to help them improve their next presentation.

If students worked on a project in a cooperative group, they should complete the Group Evaluation together. This evaluation offers students the opportunity to assess the effectiveness of their group by focusing on what worked and what might need improvement. Students fill out the form and share their responses as a group.

At the end of the unit, the students will fill out a Reflection Form to encourage individual learners to think about how and what they have learned. Students write their responses to the questions to share with the class. File evaluations for use during parent conferences.

After students finish the main assignment, you may add to, delete, or require one or more of the extension activities as part of the unit. Many of the extensions include assessment rubrics.

★ Unit Goals

Content Objective:
Understand the causes and effects of natural disasters.

Performance Objective:
Work cooperatively with a partner or a small group to research, write, and film a documentary video about a natural disaster.

Materials and Resources

 ### Main Assignment

Each student or group needs one copy of each of the following handouts:

- Main Assignment
- Graphic Organizer (2 pages)
- Data Collector (2 pages)
- Video Documentary Guidelines
- Video Documentary Storyboard (copies as needed)
- Video Documentary Rubric
- Group Evaluation
- Reflection Form

Extension Activities

If students pursue additional activities, each student will need one copy of each of the following:

Describe Natural Disasters Using Metaphors and Similes

- Picture Strip Guidelines
- Picture Strip Format
- Picture Strip Rubric

Design a Safety Poster

- Safety Poster Guidelines

 ### Internet Resources

Wild Weather:
   http:www.wildweather.com

Climactic Changes and Weather Events:
   http://www.ncdc.noaa.gov/ol/climate/severeweather/extremes.html

FEMA for Kids:
   http://www.fema.gov/kids

Student Projects

Main Assignment

Select one type of natural disaster, such as a tornado, hurricane, drought, flood, earthquake, blizzard, or volcanic eruption, and find out all you can about that disaster.

- When is this disaster most likely to happen?

- In what part of the world is the disaster most likely to occur?

- Describe the conditions of the Earth or its atmosphere that bring about this disaster.

- What type of damage does it cause?

- How can people prepare and/or protect themselves before, during, or after this disaster?

When you have finished your research, you and a partner or a small group will design and film a video documentary about the significant aspects of the disaster.

Extension Activities

After you complete the main assignment, show what you have learned by completing one of the following extension activities. Your teacher will provide more information about each activity and ask you to work independently, in a small group, or with the whole class.

1. Describe natural disasters using metaphors and similes in a picture strip format.

2. Design a safety poster that informs people about how to protect themselves and describes steps to prepare for such a disaster.

3. Other Activity: _____

6 • Natural Disasters

Name   Date

Usual geographic location

Environmental causes

Kind of disaster researched

Warning signs

Environmental effects

Graphic Organizer, Part 2

Name _____ **Date** _____

Safety measures

Before	During	After

Write a brief description of an actual occurrence of this natural disaster.
Include the date, location, and other statistical information in your notes.

_____

_____

_____

_____

_____

List authors and references used in your research.

_____

_____

_____

_____

_____

6 • Natural Disasters

Data Collector, Part 1

Name _____ **Date** _____

6 • Natural Disasters

Type of natural disaster:

_____

Geographic region in which the disaster is most likely to occur.

_____

_____

Describe the environmental causes.

_____

_____

_____

_____

_____

Describe the environmental effects.

_____

_____

_____

_____

_____

List the warning signs of the disaster.

_____

_____

_____

_____

_____

_____

_____

Data Collector, Part 2

6 • Natural Disasters

Name _____ **Date** _____

What safety measures can be taken before, during, and after the disaster?

_____

_____

_____

_____

_____

_____

_____

_____

_____

_____

_____

_____

_____

Write a brief description of an actual natural disaster. Include important statistics. (For example: Hurricane Bonnie, August 1998, struck eastern North Carolina and Virginia; approximately $1.0 billion in damage and related costs; three hurricane-related deaths.)

_____

_____

_____

_____

_____

_____

_____

_____

_____

_____

_____

_____

6 • Natural Disasters

Video Documentary Guidelines

After researching an actual occurrence of a natural disaster event, work with a partner or in a small group to create a video documentary.

- Use the Video Production Storyboard to help you plan the video.

- Speak to the audience as the narrator(s) of your disaster video documentary.

- The documentary should inform the audience about aspects of the disaster, such as cause and effect, safety procedures, reenactment of a past disaster, and so on.

- The video should have at least one special effect, such as the camera shaking to simulate an earthquake or the use of a fan to replicate tornado winds.

- Use background scenery.

- Use props and/or costumes to enhance the presentation.

- Develop a unique, creative depiction of the disaster.

Main Assignment • Video Documentary Storyboard

6 • Natural Disasters

Name _____ **Date** _____

Use the boxes below to sketch a picture of each frame of your video.
Write related information below each picture.

Description: _____

Description: _____

Description: _____

Description: _____

Description: _____

Description: _____

Main Assignment • Video Documentary Rubric

Name _____ **Date** _____

Project Title _____ **Total** _____

Circle the number of the paragraph that best describes the student's performance on a continuum of 4 (highest) to 1 (lowest).

	4	3	2	1
Content	Project demonstrates high mastery of topic. Presentation is varied and flows well. Project is unique and highly creative.	Project demonstrates mastery of the topic. Presentation is varied and interesting.	Project demonstrates limited mastery of the topic. Presentation is disjointed and hard to follow.	Project demonstrates little or no understanding of the topic. Presentation lacks cohesiveness and is difficult to understand.
Overall Presentation	Project shows high level of creativity. Presentation enhances the topic and offers original interpretation of the information.	Project is creative and interesting. Presentation is effective and inventive.	Project shows limited creativity. Presentation does show an attempt to show ideas of the topic.	Project shows lack of creativity. Presentation is fragmented and detracts from the topic.
Video Presentation	All of the criteria contained in the guidelines are presented in a unique manner.	All criteria in the guidelines are included.	Some guidelines are not addressed.	Many guidelines are not addressed.
Use of Technology	Demonstrates high level of understanding and comfort with the technology used. The video camera is used in a very effective way to communicate topic ideas.	Demonstrates understanding of the technology used. The video camera is used effectively to show knowledge of the topic.	Demonstrates limited understanding of the technology. There is an attempt to use the video camera to communicate knowledge of the topic.	Demonstrates little or no understanding of the technology. Knowledge of content is lost in the process.

6 • Natural Disasters

 Picture Strip Guidelines

Using the Picture Strip Format organizer, write and illustrate three metaphors and three similes that compare a natural disaster to other things. See the definitions and examples below.

Use the following guidelines for this project:

- Choose any of the following disasters: hurricanes, tornadoes, floods, earthquakes, blizzards, droughts, volcanic eruptions, or tidal waves.

- Make a plan on paper first, then transfer it to the printed organizer.

- In the larger boxes on the Picture Strip form, draw pictures of your metaphors and similes. Make each illustration colorful.

- In the smaller boxes, write a statement about each illustration. Be creative and use correct punctuation, capitalization, and spelling.

- The statement and picture must relate to one another.

Definitions

Metaphor: A figure of speech that compares two things without using the words *like* or *as*.
Example: She cried a <u>flood of tears</u>.
A <u>hurricane of feelings</u> swept through citizens across the country.

Simile: A figure of speech that compares two things that are not alike using the words *like* or *as*.
Example: The toddler swept through the room <u>like a tornado</u>!
His tantrum was as <u>sudden as an earthquake</u>.

6 • Natural Disasters

Name _____   Date _____

Simile	
3.	

Simile	
2.	

Simile	
1.	

Metaphor	
6.	

Metaphor	
5.	

Metaphor	
4.	

Extension Activity • Picture Strip Rubric

6 • Natural Disasters

Name _____ **Date** _____

Project Title _____ **Total** _____

Circle the number of the paragraph that best describes the student's performance on a continuum of 4 (highest) to 1 (lowest).

	4	**3**	**2**	**1**
Creative Writing	There are three metaphors and three similes, cleverly written, to express qualities of some natural disasters listed. Statements are written in the smaller boxes.	There are three metaphors and three similes correctly expressing qualities of some natural disasters. Statements appear in the smaller boxes.	Picture strips demonstrate an attempt to use metaphors and similes to express qualities of some natural disasters, but writing is confusing.	There are some statements, but they do not use metaphors and similes.
Mechanics	There is correct punctuation, capitalization, and spelling.	Punctuation, capitalization, and spelling show very minor errors.	Punctuation, capitalization, and spelling show many errors.	There is a large number of punctuation, capitalization, and spelling errors.
Illustrations	Colorful drawings illustrate the statements in a creative way. Pictures are drawn in the larger boxes.	Colorful drawings, in the larger boxes, illustrate the statements.	Drawings illustrate the statements.	Drawings do not relate to statements.
Overall Appearance	The product is neat and very attractive.	The product is neat and interesting to look at.	The product shows an attempt at being neat.	There is little or no attempt at neatness. Pictures and words are not necessarily in the right places.

6 • Natural Disasters

 # Safety Poster Guidelines

For this project, you will design a safety poster. Your poster can inform people how to protect themselves in the event of a disaster or show people how to make a disaster home safety kit. Select a natural disaster that interests you.

Follow these guidelines:

Disaster Response Poster

- Contact local and national weather bureaus or a disaster relief organization for further information about disaster preparedness. Check with your school on safety precautions currently in place and procedures to be followed in the event that this natural disaster should occur nearby.

- Create a safety poster that tells and illustrates the rules that must be followed before, during, and after this type of disaster. Be creative with art materials to make a poster that will attract people's attention.

- Write neatly and clearly so that everyone will understand your message.

Safety Kit Poster

- Create a poster that illustrates the best items to include in a disaster home safety kit. On the poster, explain why you chose the items you did.

- Experiment with art materials to make a poster that will attract people's attention.

- Write neatly and clearly so that everyone will understand your message.

Hints for Effective Posters:

- Grab the readers' attention by carefully choosing colors and style.

- Provide information in a creative way.

- Create a message that is easy to read.

- Make the message neat, clear, and easy to understand.

- Encourage the reader to take action by creating awareness and providing important information.

Group Evaluation

6 • Natural Disasters

Name _____ **Date** _____

Group Name (s) _____ **Total** _____

Fill in the blank next to each statement below with the following numbers: 4, 3, 2, or 1. Use the numbers to indicate how well the group worked together.

> **4** Very best efforts were given each time we met.
> **3** Good effort was given each time we met.
> **2** Some effort was shown, but direction was needed from outside the group.
> **1** Little effort was given to the project.

Group Members:

_____ Showed positive behavior.

_____ Cooperated by listening to each other.

_____ Shared creative ideas.

_____ Used good organizational skills.

_____ Contributed good research to develop the project.

_____ Brought and/or shared materials when needed.

_____ Cleaned up materials at the end of each work session.

_____ Produced an attractive, neat, and accurate project.

_____ Planned the presentation together, with all members taking part.

Please add any comments about the cooperative behavior of your group that you feel would be helpful for your teacher to know.

_____

_____

_____

_____

Reflection Form

Name _____ **Date** _____

I enjoyed learning about . . .
_____
_____
_____

I especially enjoyed doing . . .
_____
_____
_____

I am still wondering about . . .
_____
_____
_____

The materials in which I found the most information were . . .
_____
_____
_____

What I found most challenging was . . .
_____
_____
_____

I improved the most in . . .
_____
_____
_____

Social
Studies
Themes

7 • Ancient Civilizations

Memo to the Teacher

Before beginning research, students should choose an ancient civilization that interests them. They will collect this information on the Graphic Organizer provided. Following are some suggestions for topics:

Egyptian	Aztec	Chinese
Grecian	Native American	Japanese
Roman	African	Mayan

At the end of the research phase of the activity, students will create a Civilization Alphabet Book using the words and images they have found in their research about the civilization. This book can be created by individual students or by small groups of students who researched the same civilization. After viewing a presentation, complete the rubric provided by circling the choice in each row that applies to that student's or group's work. Meet with the student or group and share the rubric to help students improve their next presentation.

If students worked on a project in a cooperative group, they should complete the Group Evaluation together. This evaluation offers students the opportunity to assess the effectiveness of their group by focusing on what worked and what might need improvement. Students are to fill out the evaluations and share their responses as a group.

At the end of the unit, the students will fill out a Reflection Form to encourage individual learners to think about how and what they have learned. Students write their responses to the questions to share with the class. File evaluations for use during parent conferences.

After students finish the main assignment, you may add to, delete, or require one or more of the extension activities. Many of the extensions also include assessment rubrics.

★ Unit Goals

Content Objective:
Become familiar with various aspects of an ancient civilization including government, artifacts, dress and everyday life.

Performance Objective:
Create an illustrated alphabet book that demonstrates knowledge of the civilization researched.

Materials and Resources

Main Assignment

Each student or group needs one copy of each of the following:

- Main Assignment
- Graphic Organizer (3 pages)
- Data Collector (3 pages)
- Alphabet Book Guidelines
- Alphabet Book Planning Sheet
- Alphabet Book Rubric
- Group Evaluation
- Reflection Form

Extension Activities

If students pursue additional activities, each student will need one copy of each of the following:

Write and Perform a Puppet Show About the Civilization
- Puppet Show Guidelines
- Puppet Show Rubric

Design a Slide Show Presentation About the Civilization
- Slide Show Presentation Guidelines
- Slide Show Presentation Planner
- Slide Show Presentation Rubric

Design a Mural Depicting the Civilization
- Mural Guidelines
- Board Game Rubric

Internet Resources

Ancient Egypt from A–Z:
    http://www.geocities.com/ amenhotep/glossary/index.html

The Ancient World Web:
    http://www.julen.net/ancient/

Exploring Ancient World Cultures:
    http://eawc.evansville.edu/index.htm

Student Projects

 Main Assignment

You will be collecting data about an ancient civilization. There are a number from which to choose, including the ancient peoples of Egypt, Greece, and Rome, and the ancient Mayans. Do a little preliminary research in books and on the Internet before making your choice. After choosing a civilization, use the Graphic Organizer to take notes about the way people of the civilization lived.

Research the following information:
- What did they wear?
- What did their homes look like?
- What kind of government ruled them?

Use the Data Collector to expand your notes into more detailed information and to express information in complete thoughts. Use words and images from your research to create an Alphabet Picture Book about your civilization.

Extension Activities

After you complete the main assignment, show what you have learned by completing one of the extension activities. Your teacher will provide more information about each activity and ask you to work independently, in a small group, or with the whole class.

1. Write and perform a puppet show about the civilization.

2. Design a slide show presentation about the civilization.

3. Design a mural showing the people and biome of the civilization.

4. Other Activity: _____

Graphic Organizer, Part 1

Name _____ Date _____

Government

_____
_____
_____
_____
_____
_____
_____

Religion

_____
_____
_____
_____
_____
_____

Name of the civilization

_____

Dates of existence

_____

Important persons

_____
_____
_____
_____
_____
_____
_____
_____

Geographic location

_____
_____
_____
_____
_____
_____
_____

Graphic Organizer, Part 2

Name _____ **Date** _____

Housing
_____
_____
_____
_____
_____
_____

Daily Activities
_____
_____
_____
_____
_____
_____

Clothing
_____
_____
_____
_____
_____

Recreation
_____
_____
_____
_____
_____
_____
_____

Artifacts
_____
_____
_____
_____
_____
_____

Interesting facts
_____
_____
_____
_____
_____

Name _____   **Date** _____

7 • Ancient Civilizations

Compare our civilization to the ancient civilization you are studying.

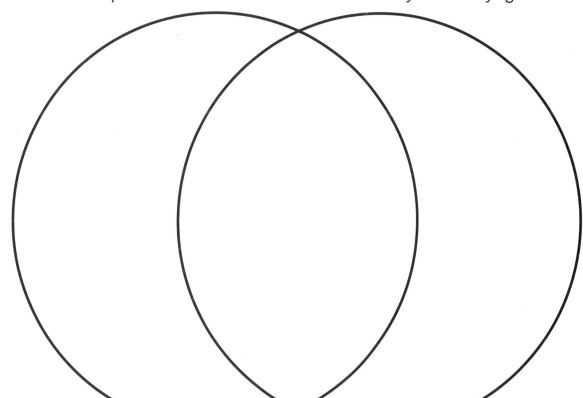

Our civilization

Ancient civilization

List your references with authors and titles.

_____

_____

_____

_____

_____

_____

_____

Data Collector, Part 1

Name _____ **Date** _____

Name of the civilization:

_____

Approximate dates the civilization existed:

_____

In which geographical area of the world was the civilization?

_____

_____

What ancient countries were included in the civilization?

_____

_____

Describe daily life.

_____

_____

_____

_____

_____

_____

_____

_____

_____

_____

_____

_____

_____

_____

Data Collector, Part 2

7 • Ancient Civilizations

Name _____ **Date** _____

How did the people support themselves and their families?

_____

_____

_____

_____

Describe the houses or dwellings.

_____

_____

_____

_____

What form of government was used?

_____

_____

_____

_____

Name a prominent person in the civilization and explain his or her importance.

_____

_____

_____

_____

What did people wear?

_____

_____

_____

Sketch the type of clothing worn by men, women, and children on a
separate sheet of paper.

Data Collector, Part 3

7 • Ancient Civilizations

Name _____ Date _____

What did the people do for recreation?

_____

_____

_____

_____

Describe the religion or rituals practiced.

_____

_____

_____

_____

What tools, weapons, and other artifacts were used?

_____

_____

_____

_____

How does the civilization compare to ours?

_____

_____

_____

_____

List two interesting facts about the civilization.

a. _____

_____

b. _____

_____

Main Assignment • Alphabet Book

Alphabet Book Guidelines

After finishing your research, create an illustrated alphabet book based on words that describe the civilization you studied. The book will serve as a glossary for the civilization. Your Ancient Civilization Alphabet Book should include the following:

1. A cover
2. A title page
3. Alphabet pages
4. A bibliography

Include a civilization-related term or artifact for each letter of the alphabet. These can be descriptive words or names of artifacts. Fill out the Alphabet Book Planner with your terms before starting your book.

Provide a short description and an illustration with each entry. Illustrations can be clip art or hand-drawn. All text entries should be word processed or neatly handwritten, and all entries should use correct grammar, spelling, and capitalization. Your book should demonstrate your knowledge of the civilization.

Alphabet Book Checklist

Use this checklist to make sure your alphabet book is finished.

_____ Book is word processed or neatly handwritten.

_____ Illustrations are colorful and appealing.

_____ Grammar is correct.

_____ Capitalization is correct.

_____ Definitions are easily understood.

_____ Punctuation is correct.

_____ Entries are spelled correctly.

Main Assignment • Alphabet Book Planner

Name _____ **Date** _____

	Illustration	Word or Artifact	Description
• Cover page			
• Letter pages			
A			
B			
C			
D			
E			
F			
G			
H			
I			
J			
K			
L			
M			
N			
O			
P			
Q			
R			
S			
T			
U			
V			
W			
X			
Y			
Z			
• Resource page			

Main Assignment • Alphabet Book Rubric

Name _____ **Date** _____

Project Title _____ **Total** _____

Circle the number of the paragraph that best describes the student's performance on a continuum of 4 (highest) to 1 (lowest).

7 • Ancient Civilizations

	4	**3**	**2**	**1**
Evidence of Research	The picture book is unique and visually appealing and shows exceptional mastery of the topic.	The picture book demonstrates mastery of the topic. It is organized and easy to understand.	The picture book demonstrates limited mastery of the topic. It is unorganized and difficult to understand.	The picture book shows little or no understanding of the topic. It is visually unappealing and difficult to comprehend.
Mechanics	The text follows correct writing guidelines (mechanics, spelling, and so on).	There are minor text errors (spelling, mechanics, and so on).	Poor writing skills are evident, including misspelled words.	Numerous errors are evident.
Content and Organization	The picture book follows all criteria in the guidelines. The text is expressive and informative.	The picture book guidelines are evident and are expressed in an easily understood manner.	Most of the criteria found in the guidelines are evident, but book is poorly organized and difficult to comprehend.	The picture book shows little or no understanding of the civilization and is difficult to follow.
Illustrations	Illustrations show high level of understanding of the topic and concepts. Exceptional use of detail, layout, and organization is evident.	Illustrations show good understanding of the civilization and its customs. They are visually appealing and expressive.	Illustrations show some knowledge of the ancient civilization.	Illustrations show little or no understanding of the ancient civilization. They are unattractive and difficult to follow.

 Puppet Show Guidelines

After researching an ancient civilization, work with your group to develop a puppet show about the civilization you studied. For example, your show might be set up as an interview in which each puppet talks about a different civilization, or your puppet show might focus on one civilization and its customs and ideas.

Create puppets from a variety of materials, including construction paper, paper bags, fabric, or others. Your puppet show should follow these criteria:

1. Include information that demonstrates your knowledge of the civilization. The puppet show should inform the audience about the civilization you researched.

2. Your puppet's clothing should reflect the clothing worn in the civilization. Your scenery and props should be related to the civilization.

3. Speak loudly, clearly, and with expression.

4. Be creative and make the presentation fun for your audience and yourself.

7 • Ancient Civilizations

Extension Activity • Puppet Show Rubric

Name _____ **Date** _____

Project Title _____ **Total** _____

Circle the number of the paragraph that best describes the student's performance on a continuum of 4 (highest) to 1 (lowest).

	4	3	2	1
Overall Presentation	The puppet show demonstrates high-level mastery of the topic.	Knowledge of the civilization is evident.	The puppet show demonstrates limited knowledge of the civilization.	The puppet show demonstrates little or no understanding of the civilization.
Style	Presentation reflects a high degree of understanding and insight.	The puppet show is easy to follow and understand.	The show is difficult to follow.	The puppet show demonstrates a lack of style and creativity.
Evidence of Research	The puppet show is unique and presents information about the civilization in an original way.	The puppet show is creative and interesting. Information about the civilization is accurate.	An attempt has been made to make the show interesting. Some information about the civilization is inaccurate.	Little or no information about the civilization is presented.
Delivery	Presentation demonstrates a keen sense of drama and timing. Presenters speak loudly, clearly, and with expression.	A sense of drama and timing are used to communicate with the audience. Presenters are easily heard and understood.	Limited understanding of drama and timing is apparent. Presenters are not easily heard and use little oral expression.	Presenters have little or no understanding of drama and timing. They are unable to make themselves heard or understood.

 # Slide Show Presentation Guidelines

After researching a civilization, use your information to create a slide show presentation that demonstrates your knowledge. Follow these guidelines to create your slide show presentation:

1. Your slide show presentation should contain at least 12 slides.

2. The first slide should contain the title and the authors of the presentation.

3. The presentation should detail at least four major aspects of the civilization, such as clothing, religion, government, recreation, and important people. Use your graphic organizer or data collector to help you.

4. All slides should contain both text and illustrations. Illustrations may be computer drawn, scanned, or clip art.

5. The presentation may contain sounds that enhance the overall presentation.

6. Each slide should have a button, and the presentation should be easy to navigate.

7. Check all text for correct spelling, punctuation, grammar, and capitalization.

8. The last slide should contain the names of authors and resources you used to find the information.

9. The presentation should be inviting, appealing, and user friendly.

Name _____ **Date** _____

7 • Ancient Civilizations

Use this sheet to help you plan your slide show presentation.

Slide # _____

Text _____

Slide # _____

Text _____

Slide # _____

Text _____

Extension Activity • Slide Show Rubric

Name _____ **Date** _____

Project Title _____ **Total** _____

Circle the number of the paragraph that best describes the student's performance on a continuum of 4 (highest) to 1 (lowest).

	4	3	2	1
Overall Presentation	The presentation demonstrates high level of mastery of the civilization researched. The presentation meets and exceeds all criteria found in the slide show guidelines.	The presentation demonstrates mastery of the topic. Presentation is varied and interesting and contains at least 12 slides.	Project demonstrates limited mastery of the topic. Presentation is somewhat disjointed and hard to follow and has fewer than 12 slides.	Project demonstrates little or no understanding of the topic. Presentation lacks cohesion and is difficult to comprehend or has fewer than 12 slides.
Visual Creativity	Project shows high level of creativity. The presentation enhances the topic and offers a detailed presentation about an ancient civilization.	Project is creative and interesting. Pictures of the houses, dress, and artifacts are vivid and detailed.	Project demonstrates limited creativity and the presentation shows an attempt to expand the ideas of the topic.	Project shows lack of creativity. The presentation is fragmented and distracts from the content of the topic.
Evidence of Research	Presentation demonstrates high-level knowledge of an ancient civilization and its people's lifestyles. The presentation flows well and tools and buttons are used correctly and creatively.	Knowledge of the topic is evident. The presentation is easy to follow and understand. Buttons and tools are used correctly.	Project demonstrates some knowledge of the topic. An attempt has been made to include the basic fundamentals of slide show design.	Project demonstrates little knowledge of the topic. The presentation is difficult to follow and understand. Buttons and tools are improperly used.
Use of Technology	The presentation demonstrates a high level of understanding and comfort with the technology used in the project. Technology is used in an extremely effective manner to communicate.	The presentation demonstrates understanding of the technology used. Technology is used effectively to demonstrate knowledge of the topic.	The presentation shows limited understanding of the technology. Technology used shows an attempt to communicate knowledge of the topic.	The presentation demonstrates little or no knowledge of the technology used. Knowledge of content is lost in the process.

Extension Activity • Mural

 ## Mural Guidelines

After researching a civilization, work alone or with other students who researched the same civilization to create a wall mural.

Follow these guidelines:

1. Use paper that is between 36 and 48 inches long. Use markers, crayons, paint, or other media to complete the mural.

2. Design a scene that depicts some aspect of the civilization.

3. Add details, such as tools or plants, to the mural to enhance its presentation.

4. Write a paragraph that gives the name of the civilization and describes in detail what is going on in the mural.

5. Make the mural informative and attractive.

Group Evaluation

Name _____ **Date** _____

Group Name (s) _____ **Total** _____

Fill in the blank next to each statement below with the following numbers: 4, 3, 2, or 1. Use the numbers to tell your teacher how the group worked together.

> **4** Very best efforts were given each time we met.
> **3** Good effort was given each time we met.
> **2** Some effort was shown, but direction was needed from outside the group.
> **1** Little effort was given to the project.

Group Members:

_____ Showed positive behavior.

_____ Cooperated by listening to each other.

_____ Shared creative ideas.

_____ Used good organizational skills.

_____ Contributed good research to develop the project.

_____ Brought and/or shared materials when needed.

_____ Cleaned up materials at the end of each work session.

_____ Produced an attractive, neat, and accurate project.

_____ Planned the presentation together, with all members taking part.

Please add any comments about the cooperative behavior of your group that you feel would be helpful for your teacher to know.

_____

_____

_____

_____

Reflection Form

Name _____ **Date** _____

I enjoyed learning about . . .
_____
_____
_____

I especially enjoyed doing . . .
_____
_____
_____

I am still wondering about . . .
_____
_____
_____

The materials in which I found the most information were . . .
_____
_____
_____

What I found most challenging was . . .
_____
_____
_____

I improved the most in . . .
_____
_____
_____

8 • Architecture

Memo to the Teacher

This unit is designed to give students opportunities to learn architectural information about a famous structure and about the architect who designed the structure. An excellent teacher resource is *Architecture in Education* (published by The Foundation for Architecture, 1737 Chestnut Street, Second Floor, Philadelphia, PA 19103; phone 215-569-3187).

A list of terms for architectural styles and elements and their definitions is provided for students in this unit. Rather than simply distributing the list of terms, you may introduce the vocabulary to students using a visual presentation, such as a bulletin board display, of labeled pictures. Students can search magazines, newspapers, or sales fliers to clip additional examples of these styles and elements to create a photo collage for each term. Another way to familiarize students with architectural terms is to take a class architectural appreciation walk in the surrounding area, and use a camera to take pictures of good examples of architectural styles and elements. As students become more familiar with these terms, you can plan matching games to practice matching the terms, pictures, and definitions of architectural elements and styles.

Students can research a historic building, monument, or other structure in your local vicinity, or you may ask them to choose from the list below:

Taj Mahal	*Sears Tower*	*Lincoln Memorial*
Empire State Building	*Sydney Opera House*	*U.S. Capitol Building*
Statue of Liberty	*St. Louis Arch*	*Hoover Dam*
Notre Dame Cathedral	*Brooklyn Bridge*	*Taliesin West*
United Nations Building	*Big Ben*	*The Louvre*
Eiffel Tower	*Great Wall of China*	*Mount Rushmore*
Leaning Tower of Pisa	*Golden Gate Bridge*	*Los Angeles Airport*

★ Unit Goals

Content Objective:
Become familiar with the historic and architectural elements of a chosen building or other structure.

Performance Objective:
Use the information gathered to write an informative report about a building or structure.

Memo to the Teacher

As a starting point, give students the list of architectural styles and elements in this unit. They can use what they learn about the elements and styles of architecture to describe the structures they chose for their reports. Students will gather their information on the Graphic Organizer. The Data Collector will be used to develop notes into more detailed information and to organize information into complete sentences. At the end of the research phase of the activity, students will write a report using their research.

After reading a report, complete the rubric provided by circling the choice in each row that applies to that student's or group's work. Meet with the student or group afterward and share what you wrote on the rubric so students know how to improve their next report.

If students worked on a project in a cooperative group, they should complete the Group Evaluation together. This evaluation offers students the opportunity to assess the effectiveness of their group by focusing on what worked and what might need improvement. Students are to fill out the form and share their responses as a group.

At the end of the unit, students will fill out a Reflection Form to encourage individual learners to think about how and what they have learned. Students write their responses to the questions to share with the class. File the forms for use during parent conferences.

After students finish the main assignment, you may add to, delete, or require one or more of the extension activities as part of the unit. Many of the extensions also include assessment rubrics.

Materials and Resources

Main Assignment

Each student or group needs one copy of each of the following handouts:

- Main Assignment
- Graphic Organizer (2 pages)
- Data Collector (2 pages)
- Architectural Styles and Elements
- Report Guidelines
- Report Rubric
- Group Evaluation
- Reflection Form

Extension Activities

If students pursue additional activities, each student will need one copy of each of the following:

Recreate the Façade of a Famous Structure
- Structure Façade Guidelines
- Façade Rubric

Write a Glossary of Architectural Terms
- Architectural Glossary Guidelines
- Glossary Rubric

Design a Dream Room Model and Floor Plan
- Dream Room Guidelines

Internet Resources

Great Buildings:
   http://www.greatbuildings.com/gbc/buildings.html
Modern Architectural Wonders:
   http://ce.eng.usf.edu/pharos/wonders/Modern/Home.html
Architecture for Kids:
   http://www.takus.com/architecture/index.html
About Architecture:
   http://architecture.about.com/mbocy.html

8 • Architecture

Student Projects

Main Assignment

Choose a building, monument, or famous structure to research. Select a structure from your area, your country, or from another part of the world. Do some preliminary research before making your choice. After choosing a structure, use the Graphic Organizer to record data about the building and its architect. Use the Data Collector to develop basic data into more detailed information and organize your information into complete sentences. Use words and images from your research to write a report about your structure.

Extension Activities

After you complete the main assignment, show what you have learned by completing one of the following extension activities. Your teacher will provide more information about each activity and ask you to work independently, in a small group, or with the whole class.

1. Recreate the façade of your structure.

2. Design a dream room floor plan and model.

3. Other Activity: _____

Name _____ **Date** _____

8 • Architecture

Name of the structure:

_____

Year of construction:

_____

Location:

_____

Function:

_____

_____

Name of the architect:

_____

Type of Architecture:

_____
_____
_____
_____
_____
_____
_____
_____
_____
_____
_____
_____
_____
_____

Two world events that occurred during construction:

1. _____

_____

_____

_____

2. _____

_____

_____

_____

Interesting facts:

1. _____

_____

_____

2. _____

_____

_____

_____

3. _____

_____

_____

8 • Architecture

Name _____ **Date** _____

Architectural elements used:

_____
_____
_____
_____
_____
_____
_____
_____
_____
_____
_____
_____
_____
_____
_____
_____
_____
_____
_____

Quote:

_____
_____
_____
_____
_____
_____
_____
_____
_____
_____
_____
_____
_____

Authors and references:

_____
_____
_____
_____
_____
_____

Data Collector, Part 1

8 • Architecture

Name _____ Date _____

Name of structure: _____

Function of the structure: _____

When was it constructed? _____

Where is it located? _____

Who was the architect? _____

Describe the style of architecture used in the design of the structure.

_____

_____

_____

List at least four architectural elements used in the structure.
Use the "Architectural Styles and Elements" handouts to help you.

_____

_____

_____

Detail three or four interesting facts about the structure and/or the architect that designed it.

_____

_____

_____

What significant world events were taking place during the time that this structure was built?

_____

_____

_____

Data Collector, Part 2

Name _____ **Date** _____

In your opinion, did world events affect the construction or design of this building? Explain.

_____

_____

_____

_____

If you could visit the structure, what would you want to look for?

_____

_____

_____

If you could interview the architect who designed the structure, what questions or comments would you have for him or her?

_____

_____

_____

_____

_____

_____

What makes this structure so special?

_____

_____

_____

Find a quote that describes this structure.
(If not available, find a quote about the same type of structure.)

_____

_____

_____

Draw a sketch of the structure on another sheet of paper.

8 • Architecture

Examples of Architectural Styles

People have built structures in numerous architectural styles since civilization began. Following is a sample list.

Greek

Roman

Gothic

Colonial

Federal

Victorian

Contemporary

Glossary of Architectural Elements

arch– semicircular shape used in bridges and buildings

arcade– a series of arches

atrium– an open court in the middle of a building

balcony– attached, elevated porch

balustrade– a railing system that includes a top rail, balusters, and sometimes a bottom rail

baseboard– border, usually made from wood used at the bottom of the wall along the perimeter of the floor

column– architectural structure comprised of a base, shaft, and capital

cornice– a horizontal projecting molding at the top of a wall, window, or column

cupola– a dome-shaped roof or ceiling

dome– a vaulted, hemispherical roof

façade– the face or front of a building

gable– the triangle-shaped part of a wall at the end of a sloping roof

lintel– a long piece of stone or wood above a window or door that helps carry the weight of the wall

molding– strips of curved or carved wood used for decoration

pediment– a stone or wooden shape, often triangular, found over a door or a window

pilaster– a supporting pillar or column a wall with a capital and a base, set partially into a wall as an ornamental design.

porch– a covered structure forming an entrance to a building

skylight– a window in a roof that lets more light into the building

wainscot– a facing for inner walls usually made of paneled wood

Main Assignment • Report

Structure Report Guidelines

The purpose of your structure report is to inform others about what you have learned about the architecture of the structure through research. Use your notes from the Graphic Organizer, sentences from your Data Collector, as well as additional visual information to demonstrate your knowledge.

Your report should include the following:

- **Title Page** – Create an interesting title for your report.

- **Body of the Text** – Write at least five paragraphs that include the name of the structure, name of the architect, location, materials, elements of structural style, and other interesting facts about the structure or its creator.

- **History** – Describe the purpose or function of the structure to civilization at the time that it was created. Did world events affect the construction or architectural design? How has the function of the structure changed over time?

- **Critique** – State your opinion about what this structure represents. How is the design of the structure representative of the people or culture of the times? Do you think that the architect successfully achieved his or her desired effect in creating the structure?

- **Visual Information** – Include visual representations of the structure.

- **Bibliography** – List your resources.

Your report should be neatly hand written or word processed. Proofread your report for capitalization, punctuation, and spelling. Edit your report to be certain that your information is complete and clear. The report should be appealing, creative, and neatly presented.

Main Assignment • Report Rubric

Name _____ **Date** _____

Project Title _____ **Total** _____

Circle the number of the paragraph that best describes the student's performance on a continuum of 4 (highest) to 1 (lowest).

	4	**3**	**2**	**1**
Content	The report contains an imaginative title that relates to architecture. Each paragraph follows the criteria given in the report guidelines.	The report meets all criteria set forth in the report guidelines.	An attempt to follow paragraph guidelines is evident, but the information is not well organized.	Little or no attempt to follow paragraph guidelines is evident.
Evidence of Research	The report reflects in-depth research and contains a correct title page and bibliography. The report is well organized and may go beyond the required number of paragraphs.	Complete information is presented in a well-organized and interesting manner.	Some attempt to present the information in an interesting manner is evident.	Information is missing or poorly organized.
Mechanics	The report reflects a unique style. Grammar, capitalization, punctuation, and spelling are correct.	The report reflects correct usage of sentence structure and grammar. Capitalization, punctuation marks, and spelling errors are minor.	The report reflects simple sentence structure with errors in grammar. The report contains many capitalization, punctuation, and spelling errors.	Incorrect sentence structure, grammar, and punctuation are evident. Spelling errors detract from the information.
Overall Presentation	The report is creatively presented. It is exceptionally neat and appealing.	The report is well presented and neatly typed.	The report shows an attempt to present the material in a neat manner.	The report is unappealing and messy.

Façade Guidelines

After researching your structure, you will create a three-dimensional façade (or front) of the structure. Then you will develop a riddle that will accompany the façade. Your classmates have to guess what your building is. Follow these guidelines for this project:

- Use foam core board, clay, poster board, or other materials to create the façade.

- The façade should look as realistic as possible. Use additional materials to enhance it with detail.

- Write clues about the building to be used in class with classmates. Read the clues before showing your façade. See how many classmates can guess the structure without a visual clue. Use the format below to help you create your riddle.

Clue Me In!

I am located in (city, country) _____ , _____ .

I was built in the year _____ , by the architect _____ .

Included in my architectural details are the following

three architectural elements:

_____ , _____ ,

and _____ .

These world events were taking place while I was being built:

_____ and _____ .

I am an important structure because _____ .

My architectural style and design could be described as _____ .

What structure am I?

_____

Extension Activity • Façade Rubric

Name _____ **Date** _____

Project Title _____ **Total** _____

Circle the number of the paragraph that best describes the student's performance on a continuum of 4 (highest) to 1 (lowest).

	4	**3**	**2**	**1**
Overall Presentation	The façade demonstrates a high level of knowledge about the researched structure. The riddle is unique and creative.	The façade follows the guidelines. The model replicates the façade of the structure. The description riddle offers important facts about the structure.	The façade somewhat resembles the structure. The riddle contains few details about the façade and its structure.	The façade does not resemble the structure at all. The riddle fails to give relevant clues.
Creative Use of Materials and Color	The façade shows a high level of creativity. The façade model enhances the study of the structure.	The façade is creative and interesting. Color, style, and artistic presentation are evident.	The façade demonstrates limited creativity.	The façade shows lack of creativity.
Evidence of Research	The façade demonstrates a high level of knowledge about architectural elements.	The façade demonstrates some knowledge and understanding of architecture.	The façade is an attempt to represent the basic look of the structure.	The façade and the riddle demonstrate little knowledge of the researched structure.
Construction	The façade is attractive and shows a high level of creativity.	The façade is attractive, pleasing to the eye and is representative of the researched structure.	The model is an attempt to replicate the front of the structure.	It is poorly constructed and messy.

Architectural Glossary Guidelines

Use your knowledge of architectural elements to create an illustrated glossary.

- The glossary should contain at least twenty elements. You may choose from or add to the list of elements included in this unit.

- The glossary should contain a definition of the element and include an illustration, photo, and/or magazine picture for each element.

- The glossary should demonstrate your knowledge of architectural elements.

- The glossary should be word processed or neatly written.

- Use correct grammar, punctuation, and spelling.

- The glossary should be well organized and appealing.

Extension Activity • Glossary Rubric

8 • Architecture

Name _____ **Date** _____

Project Title _____ **Total** _____

Circle the number of the paragraph that best describes the student's performance on a continuum of 4 (highest) to 1 (lowest).

	4	3	2	1
Overall Presentation	The glossary is unique and visually appealing and shows exceptional mastery of the topic.	The glossary demonstrates mastery of the topic. It is organized and easy to understand.	The glossary demonstrates a limited mastery of the topic. It is unorganized and difficult to follow.	The glossary shows little or no understanding of the topic. It is visually unappealing and difficult to comprehend.
Mechanics	The text uses correct writing guidelines (mechanics, spelling, and so on).	There are minor text errors (spelling, mechanics, and so on).	Poor writing skills are evident, including misspelled words.	Numerous errors are evident
Evidence of Research	The glossary contains all criteria found in the guidelines. The number of architectural elements meets or exceeds the criteria. The text is expressive and informative.	The glossary guidelines are evident and expressed in an easily understood manner.	Most of the glossary guidelines are evident but poorly organized and difficult to comprehend.	The glossary shows little or no understanding of architectural elements and styles.
Illustrations	Illustrations, photos, and/or pictures show a high level of understanding of the topic and concepts. Exceptional use of detail, layout, and organization is evident.	Illustrations, photos, and/or pictures show a good understanding of architectural elements. They are visually appealing and expressive.	Illustrations, photos, and/or pictures show some knowledge of architectural elements.	Illustrations, photos, and/or pictures show little or no understanding of architectural elements. They are unattractive and difficult to follow.

8 • Architecture

Dream Room Guidelines

After completing your research of a structure, use your knowledge to design the room of your dreams. Follow these guidelines:

• Decide what kind of dream room you want to design.

• Begin planning your dream room design by developing the floor plan.

• The floor plan should be neatly drawn according to scale.

• Use a cardboard box for your dream room model.

• The dream room should include at least five architectural elements.

• Use scrap materials to create furniture for the room.

• Include a detailed, written description of your dream room model. This can be hand written or word processed.

Group Evaluation

Name _____ **Date** _____

Group Name (s) _____ **Total** _____

Fill in the blank next to each statement below with the following numbers: 4, 3, 2, or 1. Use the numbers to indicate how well the group worked together.

> **4** Very best efforts were given each time we met.
> **3** Good effort was given each time we met.
> **2** Some effort was shown, but direction was needed from outside the group.
> **1** Little effort was given to the project.

Group Members:

_____ Showed positive behavior.

_____ Cooperated by listening to each other.

_____ Shared creative ideas.

_____ Used good organizational skills.

_____ Contributed good research to develop the project.

_____ Brought and/or shared materials when needed.

_____ Cleaned up materials at the end of each work session.

_____ Produced an attractive, neat, and accurate project.

_____ Planned the presentation together, with all members taking part.

Please add any comments about the cooperative behavior of your group that you feel would be helpful for your teacher to know.

_____

_____

_____

_____

Reflection Form

Name _____ **Date** _____

I enjoyed learning about . . .
_____
_____
_____

I especially enjoyed doing . . .
_____
_____
_____

I am still wondering about . . .
_____
_____
_____

The materials in which I found the most information were . . .
_____
_____
_____

What I found most challenging was . . .
_____
_____
_____

I improved the most in . . .
_____
_____
_____

9 • Art and Artists

Memo to the Teacher

Provide students with trade books and access to encyclopedias, videos, and the Internet so they can do preliminary research into various artists and their styles. Then ask each student to choose an artist and his or her artistic style and form to research.

Some examples of style include:
Impressionism
Realism
Renaissance
Futurism
Expressionism
Naturalism
Romanticism

Some examples of form include:
painting
sketching
sculpture
photography
weaving
kinetic art
pottery
etching

Some examples of artists include:

Edgar Degas	José de Ribera	Ansel Adams
Pierre Auguste Renoir	Charles Bird King	Pablo Picasso
Andy Warhol	Andrew Wyeth	Rembrandt van Rijn
Alexander Calder	Paul Cezanne	Frederick Remmington
Vincent van Gogh	Winslow Homer	Paul Gauguin
Mary Cassatt	Salvador Dali	Grandma Moses
Georges Seurat	Edouard Manet	Gustav Klimt
Georgia O'Keeffe	Norman Rockwell	Elizabeth Catlett
Ando Hiroshige	Romare Bearden	Claude Monet
Leonardo da Vinci	Maya Lin	Peter Max
Paul Klee	Grant Wood	Selma Burke

Memo to the Teacher

Students use the Graphic Organizer and the Data Collector to collect, develop, and organize their information. If possible, during the unit, take the class to visit an art museum or interview an art historian or curator. Your school's art teacher would also be an excellent person to interview.

After the research phase, students will use their information to write a report about their artist and his or her style and form. After reading a report, complete the rubric provided by circling the choice in each row that applies to that student's or group's work. Then meet with the student or group to share the rubric to help students improve their next report.

If students worked on a project in a cooperative group, they should complete the Group Evaluation together. This evaluation offers students the opportunity to assess the effectiveness of their group by focusing on what worked and what might need improvement. Students are to fill out the forms and share their responses.

At the end of the unit, the students will fill out a Reflection Form to encourage individual learners to think about how and what they have learned. Students write their responses to the questions to share with the class. File evaluations for use during parent conferences.

After students finish the main assignment, you may add to, delete, or require one or more of the extension activities as part of the unit. Many of the extensions include assessment rubrics.

Materials and Resources

Main Assignment

Each student or group needs one copy of each of the following handouts:

- Main Assignment
- Graphic Organizer (3 pages)
- Data Collector (2 pages)
- Artistic Styles and Elements
- Report Guidelines
- Report Rubric
- Group Evaluation
- Reflection Form

Extension Activities

If students pursue additional activities, each student will need one copy of each of the following:

Reproduce a Famous Painting or Sculpture
- Art Reproduction Guidelines
- Art Reproduction Rubric

Create a Poster Comparing Two Artists' Work
- Venn Diagram Poster Guidelines
- Venn Diagram
- Venn Diagram Poster Rubric

Present a Famous Work of Art to the Class
- Famous Work of Art Guidelines
- Student Observation Form

Internet Resources

Web Museum:
   http://sunsite.unc.edu/wm/paint
Artrageous Thinking:
   http://www.arts.ufl.edu/art/rt_room/Artrageous.html
Art History Network:
   http://www.arthistory.net/artist.html

Student Projects

Main Assignment

Choose a famous artist and research information about that artist's life, the artist's style and the art form created by the artist. Do a little preliminary research in books and on the Internet before making your choice. Find out more about artistic styles, such as Renaissance, Modern, or Abstract, and artistic forms, such as painting, sculpture, and photography. After choosing an artist, use the Graphic Organizer and Data Collector to record, develop, and organize the information about your artist. Use your data to write a report about your artist.

Extension Activities

After you complete the main assignment, show what you have learned by completing one of the extension activities. Your teacher will provide more information about each activity and ask you to work independently, with a partner, in a small group, or with the whole class.

1. Reproduce a famous painting or sculpture.

2. Create a poster comparing two artists' work.

3. Present a famous work of art to the class.

4. Other Activity: _____

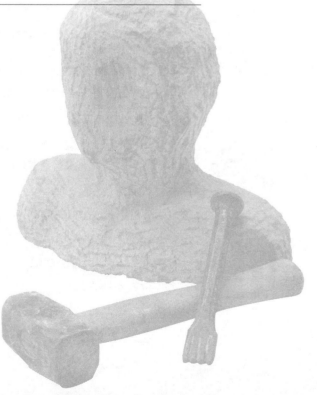

Name _____ **Date** _____

9 • Art and Artists

Artist's name:

_____

Date and place of birth:

_____

Date of death:

_____

Why this person became an artist:

_____

_____

_____

_____

_____

_____

How this person became an artist:

_____

_____

_____

_____

_____

_____

Name _____ **Date** _____

9 • Art and Artists

Some facts about artist's family life:

_____
_____
_____
_____
_____
_____
_____
_____
_____
_____
_____
_____
_____
_____
_____
_____
_____
_____

Some facts about artist's adult life:

_____
_____
_____
_____
_____
_____
_____
_____
_____
_____
_____
_____
_____
_____
_____
_____
_____
_____

Famous works:

_____
_____
_____
_____
_____
_____

9 • Art and Artists

Name _____ **Date** _____

Style, form, and media:

_____
_____
_____
_____
_____
_____
_____
_____
_____
_____

Why I chose this artist:

_____
_____
_____
_____
_____
_____
_____
_____
_____
_____
_____
_____
_____

Three important things I learned:

_____
_____
_____
_____
_____
_____
_____
_____
_____
_____
_____

9 • Art and Artists

Name _____ Date _____

Artist's name:

_____

What are your artist's birth and death dates?

_____

_____

Where was the artist born?

_____

Where did the artist live as a child and as an adult?

_____

_____

Describe the artist's family life.

_____

_____

_____

_____

How did this person become an artist?

_____

_____

_____

_____

What form and media did the artist use?

_____

_____

_____

_____

Data Collector, Part 2

9 • Art and Artists

Name _____ **Date** _____

Where did the artist learn his or her style of art?

_____

_____

_____

_____

What are some of this artist's famous works?

_____

_____

_____

_____

Which other artists influenced this artist's work?

_____

_____

_____

_____

Why did you choose this artist?

_____

_____

_____

What are three or four important things that you learned about this artist?

_____

_____

_____

_____

_____

Main Assignment • Report

Artist Report Guidelines

The purpose of your report is to inform others about what you have learned about the artist and the artwork you have researched. Use your notes from the Graphic Organizer, sentences from the Data Collector, and visual information to demonstrate your knowledge of the artist and his or her art.

Your report should include the following:

- **Title Page** – Create an interesting title for your report.

- **Body of Text** – Write at least five paragraphs of text that provide the name of the artist, his or her most famous works, information about the artist's education or training, the artist's style, and the form and media used by the artist.

- **History** – Describe the life of the artist and the factors that influenced his or her art. What did (does) the artist's work express? Explain how the artist's choice of media and style enabled his or her self-expression.

- **Critique** – Be an art critic. Write a brief review of the artist's works and the reasons for your opinions. Do (or will) the artist's works withstand the test of time? Why or why not?

- **Visual Information** – Include visual representations of the artist's works.

- **Bibliography** – List your resources.

Your report should be neatly hand written or word processed. Proofread your report for capitalization, punctuation, and spelling. Edit your report to be certain that your information is complete and clear. The report should be organized, appealing, creative, and neatly presented.

Main Assignment • Report Rubric

9 • Art and Artists

Name _____ **Date** _____

Project Title _____ **Total** _____

Circle the number of the paragraph that best describes the student's performance on a continuum of 4 (highest) to 1 (lowest).

	4	**3**	**2**	**1**
Content	The report contains an imaginative title that relates to the topic. Each paragraph follows the criteria given in the report guidelines.	The report meets all criteria set forth in the report guidelines.	An attempt to follow paragraph guidelines is evident, but the information is not well organized.	Little or no attempt at paragraphing is evident. Information is missing or poorly organized.
Evidence of Research	The report reflects in-depth research and contains a correct title page and bibliography. The report is well organized and may go beyond the required number of paragraphs.	The material is presented in a well-organized manner.	Some attempt to present the information in an interesting manner is evident.	Lack of sufficient information and poor organization detract from topic.
Mechanics	The report reflects a unique style. Grammar, punctuation, and spelling are correct.	The report reflects correct usage of sentence structure, grammar, and punctuation marks.	The report reflects simple sentence structure with errors in grammar and punctuation. The report contains many spelling and capitalization errors.	Incorrect sentence structure, grammar, and punctuation are evident.
Overall Presentation	The report is creatively presented. It is exceptionally neat and appealing.	Spelling and capitalization errors are minor. The report is well presented and neatly typed.	The report shows an attempt to present the material in a neat manner.	The report is unappealing and messy.

© 2002 Rigby

Thematic Research Projects 169

Art Reproduction Guidelines

This project gives you an opportunity to recreate something that your favorite artist once created. To make an art reproduction, follow these guidelines:

- Locate an illustration of an artist's work that you would like to reproduce. It could be a painting, a sculpture, a mobile, or other piece of art.

- Sketch the work on a piece of paper before you begin.

- List all the materials you will need. This might include large paper, chalk, paint, modeling clay, wire and sticks, or other materials. Check with your teacher for help with this list.

- Gather materials that will help you follow your plan.

- Create the reproduction.

- Include the name of the work, the original artist, and your name on an index card.

- Display your work for everyone to enjoy.

9 • Art and Artists

Extension Activity • Art Reproduction Rubric

Name **Date**

Project Title **Total**

Circle the number of the paragraph that best describes the student's performance on a continuum of 4 (highest) to 1 (lowest).

	4	3	2	1
Overall Presentation	Reproduction shows a high level of understanding about the original art.	Reproduction shows good understanding about the original art.	Reproduction shows limited understanding about the original art. Some attempt to reproduce the work is evident.	Reproduction shows little or no understanding about the original art. No attempt to reproduce the work is evident.
Evidence of Research	It is exceptionally attractive and gives the name of the work, original artist, and student(s)' name(s).	It is pleasing to the eye and gives the name of the work, the original artist, and student(s)' name(s).	It includes the name of the work, the original artist, and student(s)' name(s).	The names of the work, original artist, or student(s) are missing.
Presentation	The presentation shows exceptional attention to detail and is very well executed.	The presentation shows good attention to detail and is well executed.	The presentation shows some attention to detail. Neatness needs improvement.	The presentation shows little or no attention to detail. The project lacks neatness.
Construction and Use of Materials	Color and a variety of materials are used in a highly creative and interesting manner.	Color and a variety of materials are used.	Some color and basic materials are used. Little attention to detail.	Color or variety of materials is lacking.

 Venn Diagram Poster Guidelines

After collecting data on two different styles of painting, work with a partner to develop a poster that compares and contrasts these styles. Use poster board or paper that measures approximately 24 inches by 36 inches to display your work. Paste copies of your choices in the Venn diagram on the poster. The following picture is an example of one way to set up your information:

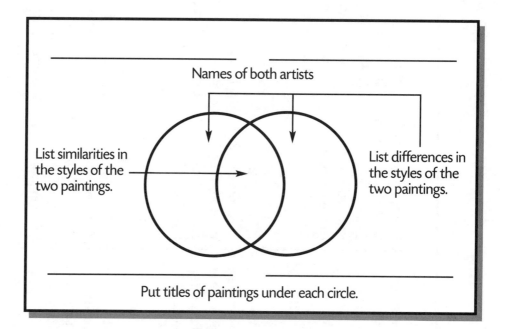

Names of both artists

List similarities in the styles of the two paintings.

List differences in the styles of the two paintings.

Put titles of paintings under each circle.

Compare the styles of both paintings by doing the following:

- Put a title at the top of your poster.
- Use pictures to show the two different pieces of art.
- List at least four differences.
- List at least four similarities.
- Word process or neatly hand write, and edit for correct and capitalization, punctuation, and spelling.
- Include a bibliography page (see Student Report Guidelines). Attach the bibliography to the back of the poster.
- Attach your Data Collector and Graphic Organizer notes to the back of the poster.

9 • Art and Artists

Name   **Date**

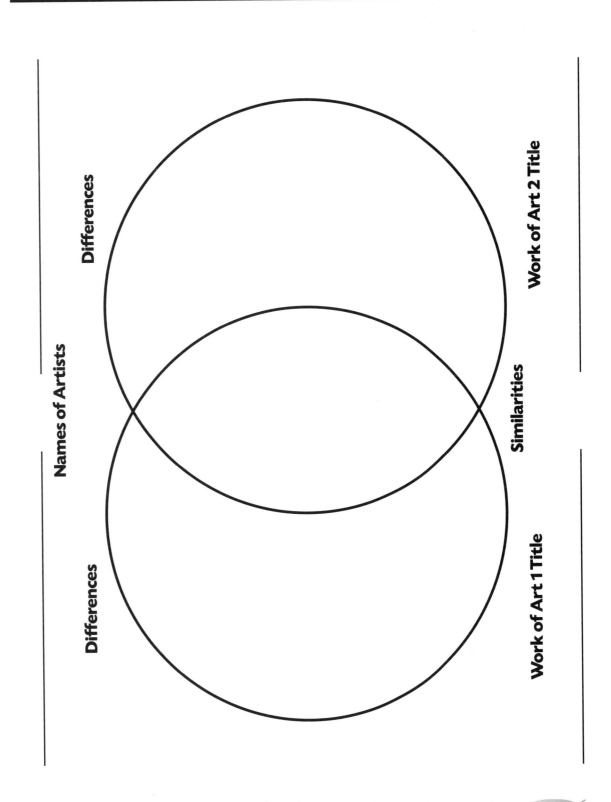

Differences

Names of Artists

Differences

Work of Art 2 Title

Similarities

Work of Art 1 Title

Extension Activity • Venn Diagram Rubric

Name _____ **Date** _____

Project Title _____ **Total** _____

Circle the number of the paragraph that best describes the student's performance on a continuum of 4 (highest) to 1 (lowest).

	4	3	2	1
Overall Presentation	Poster is visually appealing and well organized. Text is neat and correctly written.	Poster is well organized and easily understood. Text is neat with a few minor errors.	Poster shows an attempt to organize the information, but it is not easily understood. Text shows a number of errors.	Poster shows little or no attempt to organize information, as stated in the guidelines. Text is hard to understand and has many errors.
Form	Poster is properly identified, and bibliography is in correct form.	Poster is identified, and bibliography is in correct form.	Poster identification and bibliography are included but not necessarily in correct form.	Poster identification and bibliography may or may not be present.
Evidence of Research	Poster shows exceptional mastery of topics, giving four or similarities and four or more differences between the two paintings. Originality is apparent.	Poster shows mastery of topics, giving four or more similarities and four or more differences between the two paintings.	Poster shows little attempt to compare and contrast the two paintings.	Poster shows little or no attempt to compare and contrast the two paintings.
Illustrations	Illustrations are visually appealing and fit with the written information.	Illustrations complement the written information.	Illustrations are used but may not fit the written information.	Illustrations do not relate to the information or are not present.

9 • Art and Artists

 Famous Work of Art Guidelines

This project lets you concentrate on one piece of art in order to teach other people about the artist you have researched and his or her work. To get started, you will need a picture of a famous work of art to display on a piece of colored paper or poster board. Use 5-inch-by-7-inch note cards to record the important details about the work. Use the following criteria to guide your observations and form your opinions of the work of art. Locate information from various sources to support your ideas.

- Look carefully. What is the painting about?

- What style of art is used? (Renaissance, Impressionism, Abstract, Realism, other)

- What is in the picture? Name objects, people, animals, background, and so on.

- Where and when could the scene be taking place?

- What is the most important thing in the painting? Why do you think so?

- How did the artist use the following:
  - a. color
  - b. line
  - c. shape
  - d. texture
  - e. space
  - f. balance
  - g. repetition

- What media did the artist use? (watercolors, oils, photography, metal, clay, and so on.)

- Why does this work of art appeal to you?

Prepare your notes, and practice presenting your information in a creative manner. Speak loudly, clearly, and with expression. Remember to maintain good eye contact while speaking to your audience. Refer to the picture you are displaying either with a pointer or your hand. When you have finished your presentation, give your notes to your teacher.

Students will evaluate each presentation on the Student Observation Form.

Student Observation Form

Name _____ **Date** _____

Presenter(s): _____

Topic: _____

Does the group or individual presentation show originality and use its own vocabulary?
Explain. _____

_____

_____

Does the group or individual speak clearly, loudly, and with expression?
(Check all lines that apply.)

_____ Clearly

_____ Loudly

_____ With expression

Is the presentation creative and interesting?

_____

_____

Write two or more facts that you learned from the presentation.

1. _____

_____

2. _____

_____

Write one thing that your found very interesting. Then write one positive suggestion.

1. _____

_____

2. _____

_____

Group Evaluation

Name _____ **Date** _____

Group Name (s) _____ **Total** _____

Fill in the blank next to each statement below with the following numbers: 4, 3, 2, or 1. Use the numbers to indicate how well the group worked together.

> **4** Very best efforts were given each time we met.
> **3** Good effort was given each time we met.
> **2** Some effort was shown, but direction was needed from outside the group.
> **1** Little effort was given to the project.

Group Members:

_____ Showed positive behavior.

_____ Cooperated by listening to each other.

_____ Shared creative ideas.

_____ Used good organizational skills.

_____ Contributed good research to develop the project.

_____ Brought and/or shared materials when needed.

_____ Cleaned up materials at the end of each work session.

_____ Produced an attractive, neat, and accurate project.

_____ Planned the presentation together, with all members taking part.

Please add any comments about the cooperative behavior of your group that you feel would be helpful for your teacher to know.

_____

_____

_____

_____

Reflection Form

Name _____ **Date** _____

I enjoyed learning about . . .
_____
_____
_____

I especially enjoyed doing . . .
_____
_____
_____

I am still wondering about . . .
_____
_____
_____

The materials in which I found the most information were . . .
_____
_____
_____

What I found most challenging was . . .
_____
_____
_____

I improved the most in . . .
_____
_____
_____

10 • Famous Americans

Memo to the Teacher

To introduce this unit, brainstorm names of famous americans with students. They can be from the worlds of government, education, sports, entertainment, and so on. Write the names on the board, and when you have a lengthy list, ask each student to choose any three names. Have students write their choices on paper and turn them in so you can check that students have not all chosen the same three people.

Students will then read a short biographical sketch of each of their famous Americans before settling on one subject for more in-depth research. Students can use trade books, encyclopedias, or the Internet for deeper research and record information on the Graphic Organizer. Students will write a poem called "I Am" using the information they have found.

After reading a poem, complete the rubric provided by writing the number that applies to that student's or group's work in the blank next to each row. Share the rubric with students to help them improve their next project.

If students worked on a project in a cooperative group, they should complete the Group Evaluation together. This evaluation offers students the opportunity to assess the effectiveness of their group by focusing on what worked and what might need improvement. Students are to fill out the evaluations and share their responses.

At the end of the unit, the students will fill out a Reflection Form to encourage individual learners to think about how and what they have learned. Students write their responses to the questions to share with the class. File the forms for use during parent conferences.

After students finish the main assignment, you may add to, delete, or require one or more of the extension activities as part of the unit. Many of the extensions also include assessment rubrics.

★ **Unit Goals**

Content Objective: Become knowledgeable about the life of a famous American.

Performance Objective: Share information about a famous American by presenting a biographical poem and a detailed sketch of the person to be displayed.

Materials and Resources

Main Assignment

Each student or group needs copies of each of the following handouts:

- Main Assignment
- Graphic Organizer (2 pages)
- Data Collector (2 pages)
- "I Am" Poem Guidelines
- Poem Rubric
- Group Evaluation
- Reflection Form

Extension Activities

If students pursue additional activities, each student will need one copy of each of the following:

Create a Slide Show Presentation About Another Famous American

- Slide Show Presentation Guidelines
- Slide Show Planner
- Slide Show Presentation Rubric

Write a Monologue About a Famous American

- Monologue Guidelines
- Monologue Rubric

Create Models of Famous Americans

- Models of Famous Americans Guidelines
- Famous American Pattern
- Riddle Organizer

Internet Resources

Who's Who in America?:
   http://us.history.wisc.edu/hist102/bios/bios.html

A & E Biographies:
   http://www.biography.com

Main Assignment

Choose three famous Americans from a list created during the classroom brainstorming session. After reading short biographical sketches of the three famous Americans, select one for more in-depth research. Record basic facts on the Graphic Organizer. Find out more about this person and his or her life in books, newspapers, magazines, or on the Internet. Use the Data Collector to develop more complete information about your famous American. Use your data to write a poem called "I Am."

Extension Activities

After you complete the main assignment, show what you have learned by completing one of the following extension activities. Your teacher will provide more information about each activity and ask you to work independently, in a small group, or with the whole class.

1. Design a slide show presentation based on a famous American's life.

2. Write a monologue to present to the class.

3. Create models of famous Americans.

4. Other Activity: _____

Graphic Organizer, Part 1

Name_____ **Date**_____

Famous American's name:_____

Dates of birth and death (if applicable):_____
_____

Place of birth:_____

Family Life

_____
_____
_____
_____
_____
_____
_____
_____
_____
_____
_____
_____

Personal Strengths

_____
_____
_____
_____
_____
_____
_____
_____
_____
_____
_____
_____

Greatest Accomplishments

_____
_____
_____
_____
_____
_____

Graphic Organizer, Part 2

Name _____ **Date** _____

Famous Quotes

_____
_____
_____
_____

Important Influences

_____
_____
_____
_____
_____
_____
_____
_____
_____
_____

Significant Events

_____
_____
_____
_____
_____
_____
_____
_____
_____
_____

Limitations or Obstacles

_____
_____
_____
_____
_____

Data Collector, Part 1

Name _____ **Date** _____

10 • Famous Americans

Name of famous American:

_____

Record birth and death dates:

_____

_____

Where was he or she born?

_____

_____

Where did this person live as a child? As an adult?

_____

_____

_____

Tell what you know about his or her family life.

_____

_____

_____

What are/were this person's strengths?

_____

_____

_____

Who influenced or supported your famous person? How? Why?

_____

_____

_____

_____

Data Collector, Part 2

Name _____ **Date** _____

Describe the most significant events in this person's life? Why were they important?

_____

_____

_____

_____

_____

_____

What are/were the limitations or obstacles in this person's life?

_____

_____

_____

_____

What were greatest accomplishments of this famous American?

_____

_____

_____

_____

Write a famous quote attributed to this person.

_____

_____

_____

_____

Why did you choose this famous American?

_____

_____

_____

_____

Main Assignment • "I Am" Poem

"I Am" Poem Guidelines

Read a biography of your famous American. Use data from your Graphic Organizer, Data Collector, and additional research to better understand the person.

Demonstrate what you have learned about your famous American by creating an "I Am" poem. Follow the model below to create a poem on a separate sheet of paper.

"I AM"
Name of the famous American

Place of birth   *Dates of birth and death*

I am (two adjectives that describe your person).
I wonder (something about the person's childhood).
I hear (a sound or a voice from childhood).
I see (where the person lived as a child).
I am (repeat the first line).
I try (how the person made a difference in life).
I feel (feelings about an important accomplishment).
I care (people in the person's adult life, a spouse, children, or friends).
I am (repeat first line).
I worry (a problem in the person's life).
I am sad when (a sad event of the person's life).
I understand (the cause of an important event in the person's life).
I am (repeat the first line).
I say (a quote about your person or something important your person said).
I dream (a special wish your person might have had).
I hope (what the person would like to be remembered for).
I am (name of your person).

Word process or neatly write the final copy . Edit for correct capitalization, punctuation, and spelling. Your project should include the following:

- A colorful and detailed picture or other representation of your famous American.
- A title page (see "Student Report Guidelines").
- A bibliography page (see "Student Report Guidelines").
- Your Data Collector and Graphic Organizer notes.

Main Assignment • "I Am" Poem Rubric

Name **Date**

Project Title **Total**

Circle the number of the paragraph that best describes the student's performance on a continuum of 4 (highest) to 1 (lowest).

	4	3	2	1
Evidence of Research	Poem follows format and shows a good understanding of the person. It gives accurate and interesting information based on the character analysis notes and further readings.	Poem format is followed, showing a good understanding of the person. It gives accurate information based on the Data Collector and Graphic Organizer notes.	An attempt is made to follow poem format. Information about the person is inaccurate or does not follow Data Collector and Graphic Organizer notes.	Little or no attempt is made to follow poem format. Information is not accurate. Project may or may not include title page and bibliography.
Guidelines	Project includes a title page and bibliography, both in correct form. Data Collector and Graphic Organizer notes are included.	Project includes a title page and bibliography, both in correct form. Data Collector and Graphic Organizer notes are included.	Project includes a title page and bibliography but exhibits some errors. Data Collector and Graphic Organizer notes are included.	There are many errors. Data Collector and Graphic Organizer notes are missing or incomplete.
Mechanics	Poem is neatly written or word processed with correct capitalization, punctuation and spelling.	Poem is neatly written or word processed with minor errors in spelling, capitalization, or punctuation.	Poem is written or word processed with many errors in spelling, capitalization, or punctuation.	Product is sloppy with many errors in spelling, capitalization, or punctuation.
Sketch	Drawing is colorful and detailed and displays several realistic characteristics of the person.	Drawing is colorful, and displays several realistic characteristics of the person.	Drawing displays very few characteristics of the person.	Little or no attempt has been made to produce a drawing of the person.

10 • Famous Americans

 ## Slide Show Presentation Guidelines

Create a slide show presentation about one of the two famous Americans you have not yet researched. You can work alone or in a small group of two to four students combining your information on famous people to produce a larger presentation. The slide show presentation is to include six to eight important facts about each famous person. All slides in this presentation must contain meaningful pictures, an interesting background, and/or borders.

To create a slide show presentation, follow these guidelines:

> **Famous Americans Person's Name**
>
> **PORTRAIT**
> **Dates**
>
> **Presentation Designer: Your Name**

• **Slide 1:** Contains the title, "Famous Americans," the name and picture of your famous person, and dates of birth and death. Type your name as the presentation designer. You can create electronic drawings or use appropriate clip art to illustrate this project.

• **Slide 2:** Contains information about where this person was born with a drawing of him or her in a family setting.

• **Slide 3:** Contains one or two interesting facts about the person's childhood with a drawing or picture.

• **Slide 4:** Contains one or two significant events in the person's life as he or she became a young adult. Tell if the person married and had a family. Use the artwork to clarify the facts.

• **Slides 5 and 6:** Contains events and people that contributed to or supported this person's fame. Include meaningful symbols or pictures. Use animation if applicable.

• **Slides 7:** Contains the most important thing you learned about this person. Give your opinion of this person's accomplishments, and tell why you feel this way. Include a closing picture that shows your famous American as he or she grew older.

• **Slide 8:** Contains an alphabetized list of references that you used to make this presentation. This slide should contain scrolling text.

All slides should contain buttons that link the slides in the presentation and should include sound where appropriate. Your writing and art should be as creative as possible.

10 • Famous Americans

Name _____ **Date** _____

Use this form to help you plan your slide show presentation.

Slide # _____

Text _____

Slide # _____

Text _____

Slide # _____

Text _____

10 • Famous Americans

Name _____ Date _____

Project Title _____ Total _____

Circle the number of the paragraph that best describes the student's performance on a continuum of 4 (highest) to 1 (lowest).

	4	3	2	1
Overall Presentation	Project demonstrates high mastery of topic. Presentation is varied and flows well. Project is unique and highly creative.	Project demonstrates mastery of the topic. Presentation is varied and interesting.	Project demonstrates limited mastery of the topic. Presentation is disjointed and hard to follow.	Project demonstrates little or no understanding of the topic. Presentation lacks cohesiveness and is difficult to understand.
Evidence of Research	Presentation demonstrates high level knowledge of topic ideas and concepts. The presentation flows well with tools and buttons used correctly and creatively.	The presentation is easy to follow and understand. Buttons and tools are used correctly.	Very basic knowledge of the topic is presented. An attempt has been made to include basic fundamentals of slide show design.	Project shows little knowledge of the topic. The presentation is difficult to follow and understand. Buttons and tools are not used correctly.
Mechanics	Writing shows correct use of sentence structure and grammar. Writing shows correct capitalization, punctuation, and spelling.	Writing shows correct use of sentence structure and grammar. Capitalization, punctuation marks, and spelling errors are minor.	Writing shows simple use of sentence structure with errors in grammar. Many capitalization, punctuation, and spelling errors.	Writing shows a great deal of incorrect sentence structure and grammar. Capitalization, punctuation, spelling errors detract from the information.
Use of Technology	Project demonstrates high level of understanding and comfort with the technology used. The software is used very effectively to show mastery of the topic.	Demonstrates understanding of the technology used. The software is used effectively to show knowledge of the topic.	Demonstrates limited understanding of the technology. There is an attempt to use the software to communicate knowledge of the topic.	Demonstrates little or no understanding of the technology. Knowledge of content is lost in the process.

Monologue Guidelines

This project allows you to share information about a famous American by giving an oral presentation. To prepare your monologue, follow these guidelines:

- Choose one of the three famous Americans whose biographical sketches you have read.

- Study your notes from the Graphic Organizer and Data Collector so that you can speak to the audience as if you were the famous American.

- Be sure to include information that shows your in-depth knowledge of the famous American.

- The presentation should be original and creative. Props or costumes are optional.

- Practice your monologue in front of your family and/or a friend.

- Remember to speak loudly, clearly, and with expression, and make good eye contact with your audience.

- Be creative! Make the presentation fun for you and your audience.

Extension Activity • Monologue Rubric

Name _____ **Date** _____

Project Title _____ **Total** _____

Circle the number of the paragraph that best describes the student's performance on a continuum of 4 (highest) to 1 (lowest).

	4	**3**	**2**	**1**
Evidence of Research	Monologue demonstrates high level mastery of the topic. There is a high degree of understanding and insight.	Monologue shows knowledge of the topic. There is apparent understanding and insight.	Monologue shows limited knowledge of the topic. Some confusion is apparent.	Presentation shows little or no understanding of the topic.
Creativity	Monologue is unique and presents information in an original way.	Monologue is creative and interesting.	An attempt has been made to make the presentation interesting.	Monologue form is not present and there is a lack of creativity.
Style	Monologue demonstrates a keen sense of drama and timing.	Monologue shows effective drama and timing.	Monologue shows limited understanding of drama and timing.	Presentation shows no sense of drama or timing.
Delivery	Presenter speaks loudly, clearly, and with expression.	Presenter is easily heard and understood.	Presenter is not easily heard and uses little expression.	Presenter is unable to be heard or understood.

Extension Activity • Models

 Models of Famous American Guidelines

Using your research data, choose two Famous Americans and create a model for each one. Use information from research to make your models as authentic as possible.

Follow these steps to create your models:

- Choose the two famous Americans that you want to represent.

- Choose the time in history or a significant event in the person's life for which you will dress each model.

- Neatly write or word process a 5-inch-by-7-inch card for each model. On the card include the model's name, and tell why you have chosen its particular costume to display next to your model.

- Trace the model pattern on 8 inch x 11 inch paper. Design an outfit that would be appropriate for the person's time in history. Place tabs on the clothes so that they will fit on the model pattern.

- Gather materials such as construction paper, pieces of fabric, yarn, glue, and other materials to make the model and outfit attractive and authentic. Don't forget to draw the facial features.

- Cut out the patterns and clothes and dress the models. Place the cards and the models on the bulletin board, or stand them up by gluing or taping them to dowel rods.

Name _____ **Date** _____

10 • Famous Americans

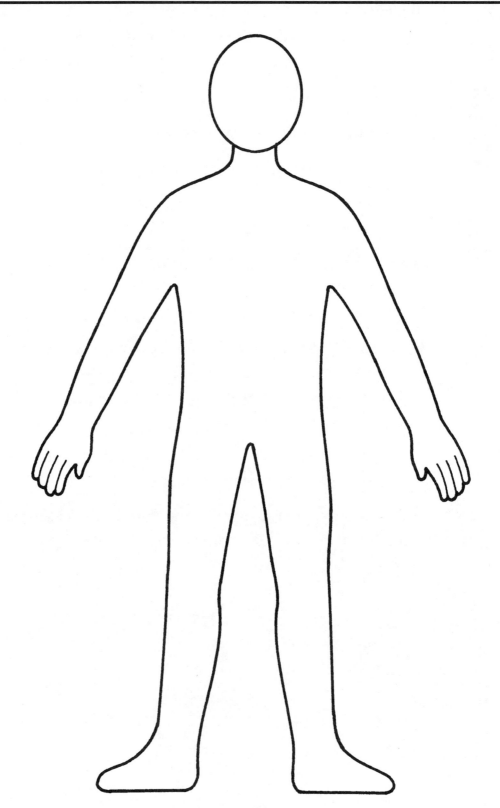

Extension Activity • Riddle Organizer

 ## Riddle Organizer Guidelines

The Riddle Organizer is designed to display important information about your famous American.

• Using research data, fill in the blanks of the Riddle Organizer with information about your famous American.

• Make a picture or model to display with the riddle. Do not show the name of your famous American. (You may choose to reserve visual clues to see if your classmates can solve the riddle based on what is written.)

• Present your "Clue Me In!" riddle to the class and let them guess the name of your famous American.

• Display your Riddle Organizer and picture or model by creating a Time Line of Famous Americans with your classmates. Arrange your famous Americans chronologically.

Name   **Date**

Clue Me In!

My place of birth was (city, state, country) _____ ,

_____ , _____ .

I was born on _____ and died on _____ ,

or I am still alive and living in _____ .

As a child, I _____

_____ .

My education included attending _____

_____

_____ .

My greatest accomplishments are/were _____

_____

_____ .

One of my most important life events was when I _____

_____

_____

_____ .

A second very important life event was when I _____

_____

_____

_____ .

A third important event was when I _____

_____

_____ .

Who Am I?

_____

Group Evaluation

Name _____ **Date** _____

Group Name (s) _____ **Total** _____

Fill in the blank next to each statement below with the following numbers: 4, 3, 2, or 1. Use the numbers to indicate how well the group worked together.

> **4** Very best efforts were given each time we met.
> **3** Good effort was given each time we met.
> **2** Some effort was shown, but direction was needed from outside the group.
> **1** Little effort was given to the project.

Group Members:

_____ Showed positive behavior.

_____ Cooperated by listening to each other.

_____ Shared creative ideas.

_____ Used good organizational skills.

_____ Contributed good research to develop the project.

_____ Brought and/or shared materials when needed.

_____ Cleaned up materials at the end of each work session.

_____ Produced an attractive, neat, and accurate project.

_____ Planned the presentation together, with all members taking part.

Please add any comments about the cooperative behavior of your group that you feel would be helpful for your teacher to know.

_____

_____

_____

_____

Reflection Form

Name _____   Date _____

I enjoyed learning about . . .
_____
_____
_____

I especially enjoyed doing . . .
_____
_____
_____

I am still wondering about . . .
_____
_____
_____

The materials in which I found the most information were . . .
_____
_____
_____

What I found most challenging was . . .
_____
_____
_____

I improved the most in . . .
_____
_____
_____

11 • Native Americans

Memo to the Teacher

Provide students with a variety of resources to allow them access to information about Native American tribes. The unit includes a Teacher's Resource List, which offers a short bibliography of books about Native American legends, and the names of the nine tribal regions that once covered North America.

Once students learn about a number of different tribes, ask them to select a single tribe for their research. Require students to submit their choices to you to ensure that a variety of tribes will be studied. Students use the Graphic Organizer and Data Collector to organize and develop the information they find.

When students have finished their research, they will complete the Canned Research Project. Students will fill a large container, such as a coffee can, with student-made artifacts that relate to their chosen tribe. Students will write paragraphs of information on various aspects of the tribe's daily life. Display the containers with the accompanying explanation on a mini-easel.

For each project, complete the rubric provided by circling the choice in each row that applies to that student's or group's work. Then meet with the student or group to share the rubric to help students improve their next project.

If students worked on a project in a cooperative group, they should complete the Group Evaluation together. This evaluation offers students the opportunity to assess the effectiveness of their group.

At the end of the unit, the students will fill out a Reflection Form. The purpose of this is to encourage individual learners to think about how and what they have learned. Students write their responses to share with the class. File these forms for use during parent conferences.

After students finish the main assignment, you may add to, delete, or require one or more of the extension activities. Many of the extensions also include assessment rubrics.

★ Unit Goals

Content Objective:
Become knowledgeable about a Native American tribal region by learning about the culture of a specific tribe.

Performance Objective:
Create a set of artifacts reflecting Native American tribal culture. Artifacts will be accompanied by a written explanation and an oral presentation.

Materials and Resources

Main Assignment

Each student or group needs one copy of each of the following handouts:

- Main Assignment
- Graphic Organizer (3 pages)
- Data Collector (3 pages)
- Canned Research Guidelines
- Report Guidelines
- Canned Research Rubric
- Group Evaluation
- Reflection Form

Extension Activities

If students pursue additional activities, each student will need one copy of each of the following:

Compare Native American Legends in an Oral Presentation
- Native American Legends Guidelines
- Legends Presentation Rubric
- Student Observation Form

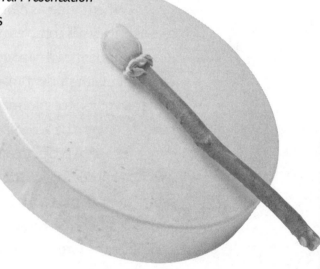

Create a Native American Diorama
- Diorama Guidelines
- Diorama Rubric

Create a Tribal Regions Map
- Tribal Regions Map Guidelines

Internet Resources

Native American Tribes:
   http://www.ilt.columbia.edu/k12/naha/natribes.html
Native American Portraits and Biographies:
   http://www.indian-history.com/bios/
A & E Biographies:
   http://www.biography.com

Teacher's Resource List

The following list of books offers information on Native American legends. Check your library for additional titles.

Baylor, Byrd. *When Clay Sings.* New York, NY: Simon & Schuster, Inc., 1987.

Bierhorst, John. *Is My Friend at Home?* Pueblo Fireside Tales. New York, NY: Farrar, Straus & Giroux, Inc., 2001.

dePaola, Tomie. *The Legend of Bluebonnet.* New York, NY: Putnam Publishing Group, 1996.

Martin, Bill. *Knots on a Counting Rope.* New York, NY: Henry Holt and Co., 1987.

McDermott, Gerald. *Raven.* Orlando, FL: Harcourt, 1993.

A list of Native American Tribal Regions of North America is provided below. Please note that labels of tribal regions differ from source to source.

Inuit	**Far North**	**Northwest Coastal**
Plateau	**California**	**Great Basin**
Southwest	**Eastern Woodlands**	**Middle America**

There are many tribes within each region, but some may not be very familiar to the students. In order to avoid frustration, guide your students to choose the tribes about which there is plenty of information available.

11 • Native Americans

Main Assignment

Take some time to read about the nine Native American tribal regions and the tribes that lived in each region. Many of these tribes still exist today. Record information about each tribe on the Graphic Organizer. After reading about the many different tribes, select one for more in-depth research. Ask your teacher to approve your choice.

Once your choice has been approved, research textbooks, trade books, periodicals, museums, and the Internet for more information. Research the following information about of the tribe:

- food
- clothing
- shelter
- transportation
- responsibilities of tribal members
- ceremonies or rituals
- other interesting information

Use the Data Collector to organize and develop more detailed information about your chosen tribe. You will use your data to complete a project to create Native American artifacts called Canned Research.

Extension Activities

Show what you have learned by completing one of the following extension activities. Your teacher will provide more information about each activity and ask you to work independently, in a small group, or with the whole class.

1. Compare two Native American legends from different tribes and present your findings to the class.

2. Create a diorama depicting daily life for the tribe you studied.

3. Create a map showing the nine tribal regions.

4. Other Activity: _____

11 • Native Americans

Name _____ Date _____

Region: _____
_____

Tribe: _____
_____

Shelter	**Food**

Name _____   **Date** _____

11 • Native Americans

Clothing

_____
_____
_____
_____
_____
_____
_____
_____
_____
_____
_____
_____
_____
_____
_____
_____
_____
_____
_____
_____
_____

Transportation

_____
_____
_____
_____
_____
_____
_____
_____
_____
_____
_____
_____
_____
_____
_____
_____
_____
_____
_____
_____

Environment

_____
_____
_____
_____
_____
_____
_____

Graphic Organizer, Part 3

Name _____ **Date** _____

Responsibilities of Tribe Members

Tribal Leaders: _____

_____

Men	Women
_____	_____
_____	_____
_____	_____
_____	_____
_____	_____
_____	_____
_____	_____

Boys	Girls
_____	_____
_____	_____
_____	_____
_____	_____

All children

_____

_____

_____

_____

Data Collector, Part 1

Name _____ **Date** _____

Name of tribe:

_____

The region of North America where the tribe lived:

_____

_____

Describe the environment of this region.

_____

_____

_____

_____

What were their shelters called, and what did tribal members use to build them?

_____

_____

_____

_____

What foods did they eat, and how did the tribe obtain their food?

_____

_____

_____

_____

Describe the tribal clothing.

_____

_____

_____

_____

11 • Native Americans

Name _____ **Date** _____

What modes of transportation did they use?

_____

_____

_____

_____

Discuss the recreational activities enjoyed by children and adults.

_____

_____

_____

_____

What types of tools were used?

_____

_____

_____

_____

How did the tribe maintain security and defense?

_____

_____

_____

_____

Describe important tribal rituals.

_____

_____

_____

_____

Name _____ **Date** _____

11 • Native Americans

List the jobs that were carried out by:

Tribal leaders _____

_____

_____

_____

Men _____

_____

_____

_____

Women _____

_____

_____

_____

Girls _____

_____

_____

_____

Boys _____

_____

_____

_____

All children _____

_____

_____

_____

Main Assignment • Canned Research Project

Canned Research Guidelines

Archaeologists and historians study objects that provide clues about ancient Native American cultures. Tools, weapons, clothing fibers, jewelry, and other artifacts provide interesting historical information about tribal life.

Think about the artifacts that might best depict the tribe you studied. Create a set of ten to twelve artifacts related to the specific Native American tribe you chose. The Canned Research Project will require you to store your artifacts in a large container, such as a coffee can or a round cereal box. You will decorate the container and create a booklet that provides an explanation of the tribal artifacts.

Research and Record

- Use as many resources as possible to find information about a Native American tribe. Write your information on the Data Collector. Your research should provide information about the following twelve topics:

type of shelters	*tribal leadership*
types of clothing	*transportation*
recreational activities	*tools used*
rituals practiced	*woman's jobs*
natural environment	*men's jobs*
foods grown or hunted	*children's jobs*

- You may also want to research Native American written language. The images used to communicate in tribal languages are called petroglyphs. You might like to use petroglyphs on the cover of your container or mini-easel.

Art of Decorated Container

- Once you have gathered information, find a large, clean coffee can or a round cereal box to use for this project.

- Cover and decorate the outside of the can so that it depicts the Native American tribe and their region. The can should have a lid to protect the materials inside. The lid can also be decorated.

Main Assignment • Canned Research Project

- Think about artifacts that would best depict the tribal culture that you studied. Design and make ten to twelve artifacts. Use a range of materials, such as paper, cloth, cardboard, pieces of fabric, and materials from nature.

Text of the Mini-Easel

- Use the information on your Data Collector to write a paragraph about each topic and about the ten to twelve artifacts from the list above.

- Write one paragraph on each sheet of 8 1/2-inch-by-11-inch paper.

- The text should be neatly written or word processed. Edit for capitalization, punctuation, and spelling errors.

- Include your Data Collectors. Be sure to include a bibliography of the sources used in your research.

Art of the Mini-Easel

Create the mini-easel:

- Punch two holes at the top of each piece of paper.

- Punch two holes at the top of two pieces of cardboard to be used as the covers of your display book.

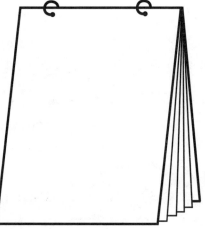

- Use two mini-rings to hold the book together, and display it as a mini-easel next to your can of artifacts.

- Decorate the cover of your mini-easel to accompany the decorations on the can. The decorated cover should include the name of the tribe, its region, your name, and room number.

- Display your completed project for everyone to enjoy.

Main Assignment • Canned Research Rubric

Name   **Date**

Project Title   **Total**

Circle the number of the paragraph that best describes the student's performance on a continuum of 4 (highest) to 1 (lowest).

	4	3	2	1
Overall Presentation	Project shows exceptional knowledge about a specific tribe. The twelve topics are creatively represented through artifacts and on the mini-easel.	Project shows good knowledge about a specific tribe. The twelve topics are well represented through artifacts and on the mini-easel.	Project shows some knowledge about a specific tribe. The twelve topics are not all represented through artifacts and on the mini-easel.	Project shows little knowledge about a specific tribe. There are fewer than twelve topics represented through artifacts and on the mini-easel.
Information and Guidelines	The mini-easel includes twelve paragraphs of information, the Data Collector, and a bibliography.	The mini-easel includes twelve paragraphs of information, the Data Collector, and a bibliography.	The mini-easel includes some, but not all of the paragraphs of information, the Data Collector, or bibliography.	The mini-easel lacks complete information, Data Collector, or bibliography.
Mechanics	It is neatly and artistically done with correct capitalization, punctuation, and spelling.	It is neatly done with only minor errors in capitalization, punctuation, and spelling.	There are errors in capitalization, punctuation, and spelling. An attempt is made to be neat	The mini-easel is not neat and has many errors in the writing.
Construction and Use of Materials	Project shows great creativity and is exceptionally attractive. It is well put together and makes use of a variety of materials.	Project shows good planning and is attractive. It is well put together and makes use of a variety of materials.	Project shows weak planning and is disorganized. There has been some attempt to use materials in a creative way.	Project shows very little planning and is unorganized. It is not attractive, nor does it use materials in a creative way.

✎ Comparing Native American Legends Guidelines

Native Americans told stories as a way to explain larger mysteries, such as *how the Earth came to be, what causes thunder and lightening,* or *why a certain animal looks as it does.* Check in your classroom, school, and public libraries for legends from two or three different tribes that give different explanations for the same natural phenomenon. See your Native American resource list for suggested titles.

After you have read the stories, prepare an oral presentation that compares how the legends are alike and different. Create a visual display, such as a poster, overhead transparency, or drawing, that illustrates your ideas and adds interest to your talk. Include the titles of your sources, the authors, and illustrators. Be sure to speak loudly, clearly and with expression. Use good eye contact with your audience.

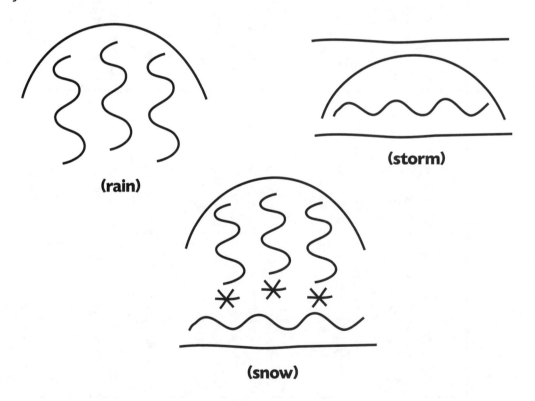

(rain)

(storm)

(snow)

Reading or storytelling one of these legends would be a special treat for the audience. You and your fellow students will observe each other's presentations and write your observations.

Student Observation Form

11 • Native Americans

Name _____ **Date** _____

Presenter(s): _____

Topic: _____

Does the presentation show originality and use its own vocabulary? Explain.

_____

_____

_____

Does the presenter speak clearly, loudly, and with expression?

(Check all lines that apply.)

_____ Clearly

_____ Loudly

_____ Expression

_____ Eye contact

Is the presentation creative and interesting?

_____

_____

Write two facts that you learned from the presentation.

1. _____

2. _____

Write one thing that your found very interesting and one positive suggestion.

1. _____

2. _____

Extension Activity • Comparing Legends Rubric

Name _____ **Date** _____

Project Title _____ **Total** _____

Circle the number of the paragraph that best describes the student's performance on a continuum of 4 (highest) to 1 (lowest).

	4	3	2	1
Evidence of Research	Presentation shows high level mastery of the topic. There is a high degree of understanding about relationships of the two or three legends of different tribes.	Presentation shows good mastery of the topic. There is clear understanding about relationships of the two or three legends of different tribes.	Presentation shows limited understanding of the topic. There is confusion about the relationships of the two or three legends of different tribes.	Presentation shows little or no understanding of the topic. Only one legend is used, and there is confusion about how ideas relate.
Presentation	Presentation is unique and presents information in an original way.	Presentation is creative and interesting.	An attempt has been made to make the presentation interesting.	There is little or no attempt to make the presentation interesting.
Visual Element	The visual is creative and adds interest to the talk.	The visual complements the talk.	Some visuals are included.	No visuals are used.
Delivery	Presenter shows a keen sense of public speaking. Presenter speaks loudly, clearly, and with expression and uses good eye contact.	Presenter shows confidence in speaking. Presenter is easily heard and understood.	Presenter shows limited confidence in speaking to a group. Presenter is not easily heard and uses little expression.	Presenter shows no confidence in speaking to a group. Presenter is unable to be heard or understood.

Diorama Guidelines

Use the information you have gathered to create a diorama of a specific Native American tribal village. Show the village environment and include people at leisure or at work.

- Use a shoebox or similar container for the diorama.

- Use construction paper, paints, crayons, markers, and other materials to make an appropriate background for the diorama.

- Make figures of clay, sticks, fabric, or other materials. Show the people involved in a leisure or work activity.

- Decorate the outside of the diorama to relate to the village inside.

- Place a 3-inch-by-5-inch card on or near the diorama to describe the scene inside. Write neatly and use correct capitalization, punctuation, and spelling.

- The finished product should be interesting and attractive. Information on the card should be accurate. Include your name and any other information your teacher requires on the card.

Extension Activity • Diorama

Name _____ **Date** _____

Project Title _____ **Total** _____

Circle the number of the paragraph that best describes the student's performance on a continuum of 4 (highest) to 1 (lowest).

	4	**3**	**2**	**1**
Overall Presentation	Diorama shows exceptional knowledge about a specific tribe and its appropriate environment.	Diorama shows good knowledge about a specific tribe and its appropriate environment.	Diorama shows some knowledge about a specific tribe, but the environment may not be appropriate.	Diorama does not demonstrate knowledge about a specific tribe.
Content	The figures show a leisure or work activity common to the tribe in an imaginative way.	The figures show a leisure or work activity common to that group.	The figures show a leisure activity or a work activity, but it's unclear as to what's happening.	There is confusion in leisure and work activities.
Explanation	The card explaining the activity is neat and correct.	The card explaining the activity is neat with only minor errors.	The card explaining the activity is not clear and has errors.	The card lacks a good explanation or is missing.
Construction and Use of Materials	Diorama shows outstanding creativity and is exceptionally attractive. It is well put together and includes a variety of materials.	Diorama shows good planning and is attractive. It is well put together and is enhanced by the variety of materials used.	Diorama shows weak planning and looks disorganized. It does not use a variety of materials.	Diorama shows very little planning and looks unorganized. It does not show good use of materials.

11 • Native Americans

 ## Tribal Regions Map Guidelines

Create a map showing the locations of the nine tribal regions in North America. Your teacher will give you a list of these regions. Your map can be made of poster board or cardboard, construction paper, fabric, clay, plaster, and any other material that is appropriate.

To get started:

• Research information about the boundaries of each tribal region. Allow for some flexibility as you may find that regions and boundaries differ slightly from source to source. Consult your teacher if needed.

• Locate the names of at least three tribes that lived in each of the nine tribal regions and write their names in the appropriate region of your map.

• Identify your sources of information on the bottom of the map.

Important details:

• Create a title for your map.

• Use a different color for each region.

• Label the regions and tribes clearly. Spell all names correctly.

• Include a map legend that explains the colors of the map.

• Include a compass rose.

• Display the map for all to see.

Group Evaluation

Name _____ **Date** _____

Group Name (s) _____ **Total** _____

Fill in the blank next to each statement below with the following numbers: 4, 3, 2, or 1. Use the numbers to indicate how well the group worked together.

> **4** Very best efforts were given each time we met.
> **3** Good effort was given each time we met.
> **2** Some effort was shown, but direction was needed from outside the group.
> **1** Little effort was given to the project.

Group Members:

_____ Showed positive behavior.

_____ Cooperated by listening to each other.

_____ Shared creative ideas.

_____ Used good organizational skills.

_____ Contributed good research to develop the project.

_____ Brought and/or shared materials when needed.

_____ Cleaned up materials at the end of each work session.

_____ Produced an attractive, neat, and accurate project.

_____ Planned the presentation together, with all members taking part.

Please add any comments about the cooperative behavior of your group that you feel would be helpful for your teacher to know.

_____

_____

_____

_____

Reflection Form

11 • Native Americans

Name _____ Date _____

I enjoyed learning about . . .
_____
_____
_____

I especially enjoyed doing . . .
_____
_____
_____

I am still wondering about . . .
_____
_____
_____

The materials in which I found the most information were . . .
_____
_____
_____

What I found most challenging was . . .
_____
_____
_____

I improved the most in . . .
_____
_____
_____

12 • Your State of the Union

Memo to the Teacher

This unit can be used for students' research of a single state or an entire region of the United States. Make available various resources for your students' research. Students can also contact local travel agencies, state representatives, or departments of tourism, agriculture, or commerce for more information.

After completing their research, students will create a standing tri-fold brochure about the state or region they researched.

Because of the nature of this research, you may want students to work in pairs or groups of three. If you choose to study the whole country as a unit, divide students into groups of five or six, each of which will study a region. Make sure that all states or regions will be represented.

After each project, complete the rubric provided. Then meet with the student or group to share the rubric. If students worked on a project in a cooperative group, they should complete the Group Evaluation together. This evaluation offers students the opportunity to assess the effectiveness of their group by focusing on what worked and what might need improvement. Students are to fill out the evaluations and share their responses.

At the end of the unit, the students will fill out a Reflection Form to encourage individual learners to think about how and what they have learned. Students write their responses to the questions to share with the class. File the forms for use during parent conferences.

After students finish the main assignment, you may add to, delete, or require one or more of the extension activities as part of the unit. Many of the extensions also include assessment rubrics.

★ Unit Goals

Content Objective:
Become knowledgeable about one of the 50 states.

Performance Objective:
Create and display a stand-up travel brochure that demonstrates knowledge of a state.

Main Assignment

Each student or group needs one copy of each of the following handouts:

- Main Assignment
- Data Collector (3 pages)
- Brochure Guidelines
- Brochure Layout Form (4 pages)
- Brochure Rubric
- Group Evaluation
- Reflection Form

 ## Extension Activities

If students pursue additional activities, each student will need one copy of each of the following:

Produce a Video about a Historical Event
- Video Guidelines
- Video Storyboard
- Video Rubric

Create a Mural of a Geographic Region
- Mural Guidelines
- Mural Rubric

Create a State Product Map
- Product Map Guidelines

Internet Resources

States and Capitals:
   http://www.50states.com/

Explore the States:
   http://www.americaslibrary.gov/cgi-bin/page.cgi/es

Stately Knowledge:
   http://www.ipl.org/youth/stateknow

Student Projects

 Main Assignment

Choose a state that interests you. Is there a state of the United States that you have always wanted to visit? What would you like to know about that state? Perhaps you have visited a place that you would like to research.

Ask your teacher to approve your choice. Then research textbooks, trade books, travel magazines, brochures, and the Internet for more information about your state. Use the Data Collector to organize and develop information about your state. You will use this data to write and design a brochure about it

Extension Activities

After you complete the main assignment, show what you have learned by completing one of the following extension activities. Your teacher will provide more information about each activity and ask you to work independently, in a small group, or with the whole class.

1. Produce a video about a historic event that happened in your chosen state.

2. Design a mural depicting a geographic scene from your state.

3. Create a map showing the products of your chosen state.

4. Other Activity: _____

Data Collector, Part 1

Name _____ **Date** _____

The state of _____ entered the United States in the year _____.

Four state symbols are: _____

_____

_____

Describe the geography of the state.

_____

_____

_____

_____

_____

_____

_____

Three of this state's major cities, by population, are:

1. _____

located in _____.

2. _____

located in _____.

3. _____

located in _____.

Three important structures are:

1. _____

located in _____.

2. _____

located in _____.

3. _____

located in _____.

12 • Your State of the Union

Name _____ Date _____

Three special attractions, such as vacation areas, theme parks, and sports teams, are:

1. _____

located in _____ .

2. _____

located in _____ .

3. _____

located in _____ .

Three well-known people from this state are:

1. _____

who lived in _____

during _____

was important because _____ .

2. _____

who lived in _____

during _____

was important because _____ .

3. _____

who lived in _____

during _____

was important because _____ .

Three important plants are:

1. _____

2. _____

3. _____

Draw the shape of the state on a separate piece of paper.

Data Collector, Part 3

12 • Your State of the Union

Name _____ **Date** _____

Three important animals found in this state are:

1. _____

2. _____

3. _____

State parks or national parks or monuments in this state are:

1. _____

2. _____

3. _____

The first park is located _____ .

The second park is located _____ .

The last park is located _____ .

Three recreational opportunities (for example, hiking, boating, skiing, surfing, and so on):

1. _____

2. _____

3. _____

You can enjoy the first one at _____

_____ .

The second one can be enjoyed at _____

_____ .

The last one can be enjoyed in _____

_____ .

The climate of the state ranges from _____

to _____ .

The weather is usually _____ during the summer,

_____ during the fall,

_____ during the winter and

_____ in the spring.

Brochure Guidelines

Create a brochure that informs people about your state and encourages them to visit that state.

To create your brochure, follow these steps:

1. Research and take notes about your state according to the topics on the Data Collector. Helpful resources include textbooks, trade books, magazines, videos, encyclopedias, and the Internet. Ask your school librarian to help you search the Internet for addresses to contact the state's departments of tourism, commerce, or agriculture. These state offices will usually send packets of information about the state. Write a letter to invite guest speakers, such as a state representative or a travel agent, to visit the class to talk about your state.

2. When you have completed your research, create a stand-up, tri-fold cardboard brochure on which to display your information. First, create the brochure itself. To do so, find a piece of cardboard that is 2 feet by 4 feet. Large cardboard boxes cut in half work well. The following diagram shows how you will identify each panel of the brochure:

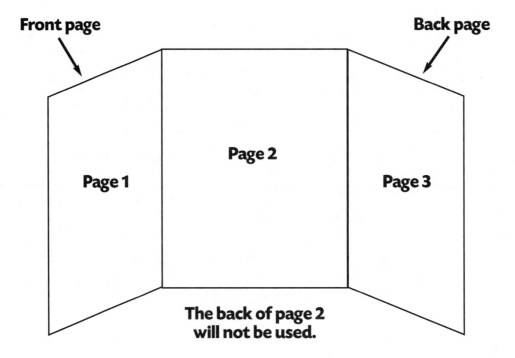

Front page

Back page

Page 1

Page 2

Page 3

The back of page 2 will not be used.

Main Assignment • Brochure

3. Once you have made your cardboard tri-fold, organize your information for display. For this task you will need the four Brochure Layout forms. The first three forms show a standard layout for the brochure; the last one gives you additional topics that you can research and display on the brochure. Use the information on your Data Collector to fill out the Brochure Layout forms. Keep in mind the following points as you work on your brochure:

- Look at professional travel brochures about your state before completing your layout. What creative touches do the brochures include?

- Your state brochure must show information about the entire state.

- The front page of the brochure should include your name, your teacher's name, and any other information that your teacher requires.

- Use the Brochure Layout forms to help you provide complete information. Be creative in the design of each page. Keep in mind that the purpose of the brochure is to attract visitors to your state.

- The brochure must be neatly handwritten or word processed with colorful illustrations that help clarify the information. Edit for capitalization, punctuation, and spelling errors. Proofread to be certain that it can be clearly understood.

- The brochure must be interesting, attractive, and neat.

- Display the brochure for prospective tourists to read.

Name   **Date**

12 • Your State of the Union

Write notes and sketch ideas in these frames.

Page 1 includes:

• The state capital and location

• Three major cities based on population size, including the location of each

Front page includes:

• State name, an outline of state, and the year that it became a state

• At least four state symbols on this page

• Your name, teacher's name, and any other information that your teacher requires

Name _____ **Date** _____

Write notes and sketch ideas in these frames.

12 • Your State of the Union

Page 3 includes:

• Three special attractions such as vacation areas, theme parks, or sports teams and their locations

Page 2 includes:

• Three important structures or monuments and their locations

12 • Your State of the Union

Name _____ **Date** _____

Write notes and sketch ideas in these frames.

The back page includes information on three well-known people from this state.

Name:

When and where did this person live?

Why is this person important?

Name:

When and where did this person live?

Why is this person important?

Name:

When and where did this person live?

Why is this person important?

Name　　　　　　　　　　　　　　　　**Date**

12 • Your State of the Union

Write notes and sketch ideas in these frames.

Additional ideas you may choose to include in the pages of the brochure:

- Three recreational opportunities and their locations:

- Climate and weather of the area:

- State flora and fauna

  Three plants:

  Three animals:

- Three state or national parks or monuments and their locations:

12 • Your State of the Union

Name _____ **Date** _____

Project Title _____ **Total** _____

Circle the number of the paragraph that best describes the student's performance on a continuum of 4 (highest) to 1 (lowest).

	4	3	2	1
Overall Presentation	Project demonstrates high level of mastery of topic.	Project demonstrates good mastery of topic.	Project demonstrates limited mastery of the topic.	Project demonstrates limited or no understanding of the topic.
Content Guidelines	Presentation is varied and flows well. Project is unique and highly creative. All elements of the guidelines are included.	Presentation is varied and interesting. All elements of the guidelines are included.	Presentation is disjointed and hard to follow. Some elements of the guidelines are not addressed.	Presentation lacks cohesion and is difficult to understand. Many elements of the guidelines are not addressed.
Brochure	Project shows high level of creativity. Presentation enhances the topic and offers original interpretation of the information.	Project is creative and interesting. Visuals are effectively used and presented in an inventive manner.	Project shows limited creativity. Presentation does show an attempt to address the topic.	Project demonstrates little or no understanding of the topic.
Mechanics	There are no errors in capitalization, punctuation, or spelling.	There are minor errors in spelling, punctuation, or capitalization.	There are a number of errors in capitalization, punctuation, or spelling.	There are numerous errors in capitalization, punctuation, or spelling.

Extension Activity • Video

 Video Guidelines

Working in groups of four, research an important historical event that took place in your state and create a ten-minute video about that event. Use storyboards for notes and to plan the presentation. To create your video, follow these guidelines:

- Use the Video Production Storyboard forms to help plan your video. Sketch each scene in a frame as you want it to appear in the video and write the narration to describe the scene as it is shown.

- Create an introduction for your video that includes a clever title, the names of the people in your group, your teacher's name, and the date of the presentation.

- Tell where and when the historical event took place.

- Tell why the event was important to your state and the country.

- Deliver the information in a creative and original manner.

- Use props and/or costumes to enhance the production.

- Speak clearly and loudly, facing the camera.

- Each member of the group should appear in the production.

Name _____ **Date** _____

12 • Your State of the Union

Draw a picture and write the narration of each frame of your video.

Description:

Description:

Description:

Description:

Description:

Description:

Extension Activity • Video Rubric

Name _____ **Date** _____

Project Title _____ **Total** _____

Circle the number of the paragraph that best describes the student's performance on a continuum of 4 (highest) to 1 (lowest).

	4	3	2	1
Overall Presentation	Project demonstrates high level of mastery of topic. Presentation is varied and flows well.	Project demonstrates good mastery of topic. Presentation is varied and interesting.	Project demonstrates limited mastery of the topic. Presentation is disjointed and hard to follow.	Project demonstrates limited or no understanding of the topic. Presentation lacks cohesion and is difficult to understand.
Organization and Mechanics	Project is unique and highly creative. All elements of the guidelines are included. There are no errors in grammar in the narration and/or the dialogue.	Project is creative and interesting. All elements of the guidelines are included. There are minor grammatical errors in narration and/or dialogue.	Project shows limited creativity. Elements of the guidelines are not addressed. There are a number of grammatical errors in the narration and/or the dialogue.	Many elements of the guidelines are not addressed. There are numerous grammatical errors in the narration and/or the dialogue.
Evidence of Research	Project shows high level of creativity. Presentation enhances the topic and offers original interpretation of the information.	Project shows clear understanding of the topic. Visuals are effectively used and presented in an inventive manner.	Presentation does show an attempt to address the topic.	Project demonstrates little or no understanding of the topic.
Use of Technology	The video is smooth, demonstrating a high level of comfort with the features of the video camera.	The video is mostly smooth, with very few jerky starts, stops, and edits, demonstrating a level of comfort with the features of the video camera.	The video has a number of jerky starts, stops, and edits, demonstrating a level of experimentation with the features of the video camera.	The video may be difficult to view, with numerous starts, stops, and edits, or the narration and/or dialogue can't be heard.

Mural Guidelines

Working in groups of three or four, research the geographical regions of your state and create a mural to depict those regions. To get started, assign a geographic region of your state to each member of the group. Each student should find information about his or her region.

Follow these guidelines to help create the group's mural:

- List the major landforms and bodies of water in each region.

- Create a blueprint of how you will show the variety of land formations and bodies of water in your state.

- Include important plants and animals in their environments.

- Make labels to identify the items displayed in the mural.

- List all the materials you will need to create a three-dimensional (3-D) effect. Use materials such as pipe cleaners, tissue paper, cotton, and construction paper. Be creative.

- You will need a large piece of paper that measures about 2 feet by 3 feet for the background.

- Once you have gathered the materials, decide what jobs each member of the group will carry out and assign a portion of the mural to each person.

- With the gathered materials, create your section of the mural based on your knowledge of the region you researched. Information should be accurate, and the mural should be neat and attractive.

- Remember to include all of your names on the project.

Extension Activity • Mural Rubric

Name _____ **Date** _____

Project Title _____ **Total** _____

Circle the number of the paragraph that best describes the student's performance on a continuum of 4 (highest) to 1 (lowest).

	4	3	2	1
Overall Presentation	Mural shows correct geographic regions of the state.	Mural shows correct geographic regions of the state.	Mural does not correctly show all geographic regions of the state.	Mural does not display geographic regions of the state.
Evidence of Research	It includes appropriate landforms, bodies of water, plants, and animals in a realistic way.	It includes appropriate landforms, bodies of water, plants, and animals.	It includes few landforms, bodies of water, plants, or animals.	It includes very few landforms, bodies of water, plants, or animals.
Labels	All labels are correct	All labels are correct.	Labels are present, but not necessarily correct.	Labels are not present.
Construction and Use of Materials	Mural shows outstanding creativity and is exceptionally attractive. It is well put together and is enhanced by the variety of materials used.	Mural shows good planning and is attractive. It is well put together and is enhanced by the variety of materials used.	Mural shows weak planning and looks unorganized. It does not use a variety of materials.	Mural shows very little planning and looks unorganized. It does not show good use of materials.

12 • Your State of the Union

Product Map Guidelines

The following steps will help you plan and create an outline map of your state that includes pictures of the important products and natural resources found in your state.

● Use atlases, encyclopedias, textbooks, and other sources to locate information about the important products and natural resources of your state.

● List at least four important examples of each of the following:
  – Farm and/or ranch products
  – Natural resources
  – Manufactured products

● Create a large outline of your state on an 18-inch-by-12-inch piece of paper. Trace the outline from a published map for accuracy.

● Draw or use cut out pictures of the resources and products you have listed. Glue them neatly on your map outline in the correct areas of the state. Check your information for accuracy. Artwork can be added in such a way as to make this a three-dimensional map.

● Be sure to include a title and a legend for your map.

● Your product map should be informative, neat, and attractive to the viewer.

● Remember to write your name on the project.

● Display your map when it is finished so that other students can learn about your state.

Cooperative Group Evaluation

Name _____ **Date** _____

Group Name (s) _____ **Total** _____

Fill in the blank next to each statement below with the following numbers: 4, 3, 2, or 1. Use the numbers to indicate how well the group worked together.

> **4** Very best efforts were given each time we met.
> **3** Good effort was given each time we met.
> **2** Some effort was shown, but direction was needed from outside the group.
> **1** Little effort was given to the project.

Group Members:

_____ Showed positive behavior.

_____ Cooperated by listening to each other.

_____ Shared creative ideas.

_____ Used good organizational skills.

_____ Contributed good research to develop the project.

_____ Brought and/or shared materials when needed.

_____ Cleaned up materials at the end of each work session.

_____ Produced an attractive, neat, and accurate project.

_____ Planned the presentation together, with all members taking part.

Please add any comments about the cooperative behavior of your group that you feel would be helpful for your teacher to know.

_____

_____

_____

_____

Reflection Form

Name _____ Date _____

I enjoyed learning about . . .
_____
_____
_____

I especially enjoyed doing . . .
_____
_____
_____

I am still wondering about . . .
_____
_____
_____

The materials in which I found the most information were . . .
_____
_____
_____

What I found most challenging was . . .
_____
_____
_____

I improved the most in . . .
_____
_____
_____